SEX AND MATH
IN HARVARD YARD

SEX
AND
MATH
IN
HARVARD
YARD

THE MEMOIRS OF JAMES MILL PEIRCE
A FICTIONAL BIOGRAPHY BY HUBERT KENNEDY

LETHE PRESS
AMHERST, MA

Published by LETHE PRESS
lethepressbooks.com

Copyright © 2000, 2008, 2019 Hubert Kennedy
This edition published in 2019

ISBN: TK
A full publication history appears at the end of the book, constituting
an extension of the copyright details.

Library of Congress Cataloging-in-Publication Data
available on request

Cover and Interior design
by INKSPIRAL DESIGN

FOREWORD

"HE WAS SOON moaning as his cock swelled larger. When it could not become larger, it became harder. With a groan, he climaxed and I felt the spurt . . ."

I could hardly believe my eyes. Was this really the secret "sex diary" of the respectable Harvard mathematician, whose professional life I had researched for several years? And yet, there could be no doubt that it was authentic—by now I knew his handwriting only too well.

This was only one of the treasures that my friend Asa had uncovered. With it was the autobiography of this true son of Harvard, who was "almost the father" of the Graduate School. It traced not only his professional development, but also—and this was why he wrote it—the development of his ideas on sex and love, revealing him to be a man ahead of his time in America and acquainted with several of the more advanced European thinkers on homosexuality. Though from a not too distant past—he died in 1906—his was a unique voice, and he deliberately wished to speak to us. He must have felt an enor mous desire to offer hope and encouragement to another generation. I did not hesitate to give up my earlier project of a scientific biography, for it seemed to me more compelling to let this poignant and passionate, restrained and yet intimate voice from the past tell his own story—in the memoirs of James Mills Peirce.

Peirce's advanced views on homosexuality, expressed in a letter to John Addington Symonds, had already been published in 1897, but anonymously. Peirce rejected the current view that homosexuality was a sin and a sickness; rather, "it has long been my settled conviction that no breach of morality is involved in homosexual love; that, like every other passion, it tends, when duly understood and controlled by spiritual feeling, to the physical and moral health of the individual & the race."[1]

If Peirce's views on homosexuality were ahead of their time, his contribution to mathematics was almost the opposite. When he began his nearly fifty years of service to Harvard University he was caught up in the current enthusiasm for quaternions, whose study had been championed by his father, himself a Harvard professor and the foremost American mathematician of his day. By the time Peirce died he was considered "the world's authority on quaternions," but by then the popularity of that esoteric mathematical theory had passed. (The theory was never disproved, it simply went out of fashion.)

Peirce's greatest academic contribution was in administration, not only as head of the Mathematics Department of Harvard University following the death of his father, but more importantly as head of the graduate program from its founding in 1872 and its first dean on reorganization as the Graduate School in 1890.

All these activities are mentioned in his memoirs, but only as background to his personal development, especially his evolving view of his own homosexuality, which is illustrated by a variety of

---

[1] The entire "Letter from Professor X." is in Chapter 10; see Appendix B for publication information. That Peirce was its true author was first suggested by Jonathan Ned Katz in his *Gay American History: Lesbian and Gay Men in the U.S.A.* (New York: Thomas W. Crowell, 1976), p. 629.

HUBERT KENNEDY

quite explicit sex scenes. But this is not a "coming out" story in the modern sense. Rather, it reads like a *Bildungsroman* in the nineteenth century tradition, only—and here it differs from the usual novels of that type—with an emphasis on sex.

Not that Peirce was obsessed with sex. On the contrary, his enthusiasms were many, and his passion for music and the stage matched that of any "opera queen" of today. He was a seasoned traveler to Europe, where he frequented the opera houses of London and Paris and attended the Wagner festivals in Bayreuth and Munich. He was also a gourmet who knew, for example, how to appreciate fresh caviar, which he tasted in St. Petersburg.

Here, then, is Peirce's story in his own words, as told in the memoirs that came to light so miraculously. My editing has been light and consisted mostly of deciding which docu ments—letters, etc.— were to be included. (Letters *from* Peirce are as they appear in his several draft letter books.) On the other hand, I thought it useful to add notes identifying the persons mentioned in Peirce's narrative, for many of them were prominent figures of the day. To round out the picture, I have added three appendices, which include a list of his publications and, for the curious, a brief introduction to the mathematical theory of quaternions.

If the list of his publications seems short on mathematics, this does not reflect his real ability; Peirce's energies were devoted to his students and to administration. As head of the Mathematics Department and Graduate School, he presided over the end of an era and ushered in the new. He was probably the last mathematics professor at Harvard *not* to hold a Ph.D.

Hubert Kennedy

ONE
THE MEMOIRS BEGIN

WHAT A YEAR 1897 has been! So many and so significant events have occurred that I really feel an era is ending—and another beginning. Most gratifying for me is my brother Bert's appointment as First Secretary of Embassy in St. Petersburg. It confirms my confidence in him; and I'm delighted that things have worked out so well for him.[1]

I'm also pleased that dear Tom is back; I have missed him greatly in recent years. His return has been the year's Great Event for *me*. Just knowing he was "here" has been a comfort; and how comfortable we have become! There is no question but that Tom has been the most important person in my life; I don't know what I should have become with out him. I sometimes think I am still deeply in love with him; at least I still think him as handsome as ever. I do hope he will stay.[2]

---

[1] Herbert Henry Davis Peirce (1849–1916). "In 1894 he was appointed by Pres. Cleveland secretary of legation at St. Petersburg, Russia, and when the legation was advanced to be an embassy and Ethan Allen Hitchcock was made the first ambassador in 1897, Mr. Peirce was appointed first secretary. He held the position for four years and became well known as an authority on Russian affairs." *The National Cyclopedia of American Biography*, vol. 9 (New York: James T. White & Co., 1907), pp. 539–540.

[2] Thomas Sergeant Perry (1845–1928). Contrary to Peirce's hope, Perry's stay was short. "Between Perry's return to Boston in July, 1897, and his departure in April, 1898, for a teaching position in Tokyo, only eight months intervened." Virginia Harlow, *Thomas Sergeant Perry: A Biography* (Durham, NC: Duke University Press, 1950), p. 166. Perry held the position of professor of English literature at Keiogijuku University in Tokyo until 1901, when he returned to Boston.

On a more prosaic note, mathematics also appears to be moving into a new era of cooperation with the First International Congress of Mathematicians in Zurich. President Eliot suggested that I go; but it really was impossible to get away. Peano was in fine form, I hear, but said nothing about the future of quaternions.[3]

A new era in the understanding of sexuality could—but I fear won't—begin with the publication of *Sexual Inversion* by Havelock Ellis and John Addington Symonds. Ellis sent me a copy of the first edition, the one with Symonds's name on the title page, before it was suppressed—with no comment! Symonds had asked him to send it. How daring Symonds thought he was to include my letter. But, as with every progressive idea he presented, he managed to hedge it so, that anyone prejudicially inclined would feel completely justified in rejecting it. A bit more openness on his part would have had better results. No wonder old Whitman insisted to him that there was nothing "morbid" or "damnable" in his Calamus poems. Of course, Walt has his own poetic obfuscations; and no doubt there is much *behind* those "Calamus" letters to Peter Doyle, which he published this year.[4] At any rate, his "Calamus" *poems* will surely have a more liberating effect on the sexes than Symonds's eternal caution.[5]

I should like to make a contribution to the understanding of homosexuality. (I do not like that word, but it appears to be the most

---

[3] Giuseppe Peano (1858–1932). In the *Rivista di Matematica* of 1895 Peano "announced the formation of the International Association for Promoting the Study of Quaternions and Allied Systems of Mathematics, and in 1901 he was National Secretary for Italy." Hubert Kennedy, *Peano: Life and Works of Giuseppe Peano*, Definitive Edition (Concord, CA: Peremptory Publications, 2006), p. 31.

[4] Walt Whitman, *Calamus: A Series of Letters Written During the Years 1868–1869 by Walt Whitman to a Young Friend, Peter Doyle* (New York, 1897). On Whitman's relationship with Doyle see *Calamus Lovers: Walt Whitman's Working-Class Camerados*, edited with introductions and commentaries by Charley Shively (San Francisco: Gay Sunshine Press, 1987).

[5] John Addington Symonds (1840–1893), English poet, essayist, and literary historian, has, oddly, acquired a reputation as an "outspoken proponent of sexual freedom." *The Alyson Almanac* (Boston: Alyson, 1989), p. 190.

neutral word available; "sexual inversion" is hardly better.) What is wanted, it seems to me, is something to counter those dreadful "case histories" in Krafft-Ebing's *Psychopathia sexualis*.[6] Although I cannot publish my own story now, I do think it could be useful to *future* generations. I have therefore determined to present myself in a sort of "memoirs"—not an autobiography—which will include a variety of items. I plan, then, to gather my personal and related items together: correspondence, diaries, notes, newspaper clippings, etc. I shall then put all of them in one place for safekeeping. No publisher would touch them now, but perhaps in fifty years a sympathetic editor may be found, who is willing to present my memoirs in an acceptable way.

One more event of 1897 must be mentioned. As I write, the great Coquelin is opening in a new play in Paris, called *Cyrano de Bergerac*. I wonder if that will not turn out to be *the* event of 1897. How I wish I could see that great actor again![7]

James Mills Peirce
Cambridge, Mass., December 28, 1897

---

6 Richard von Krafft-Ebing, *Psychopathia sexualis, mit bes. Berücksichtigung d. konträren Sexualempfindung* (Stuttgart: Enke, 1886). The seventh edition of this perennial best-seller was translated by Charles Gilbert Chaddock and published as *Psychopathia Sexualis, with special reference to Contrary Sexual Instinct* (Philadelphia and London: F. A. Davis, 1893).
7 In fact, the production of Edmond Rostand's "heroic comedy" *Cyrano de Bergerac* (Théâtre de la Porte Saint-Martin, 28 December 1897), with Benoît Constant Coquelin (1841–1909) in the title role, was a triumph.

TWO
HARVARD YARD

ONE OF MY earliest memories is the arrival of my brother Charles in September 1839, when I was a bit more than five years old. My other two brothers also arrived at five-year intervals. Our sister Helen was not part of this pattern; she intruded between the last two boys. She definitely fit into the pattern of our names, however, for we were all called by diminutives: Jimmie, Charlie, Benjie, Lellie, and Bertie. I resented the intrusion of Charles into my life, for I no longer had the undivided attention of Mother and Father. Indeed, I think Father favored Charles from the beginning. In time I came to accept that, though I often resented the fact that   Father *expected* more of him while he *demanded* more of me. Later on we dropped the diminutive endings from our names, though we did keep the usual nicknames.

My childhood was uneventful. I must have had the usual curiosity about matters sexual, but do not recall being either surprised or shocked by the things I learned. I believe I discovered masturbation for myself about the age of fourteen, and was only surprised that I did not know of it earlier. The sensations were so pleasant, how could I not have found out about them before then? For a while I made a practice of regular masturbation, almost as if I had to make up for lost time; later it did not seem so pressing. I do not recall associating sexual feelings with other boys (or with girls). Once a nineteen-year-old cousin visited us overnight and slept in my bed with me—I must have been around twelve at the time. I remember that we embraced and kissed. I greatly enjoyed it; but I already felt instinctively that I should not talk about it with anyone. Nor did my cousin say anything to me the next day about our activity. I longed to repeat the experience, but, alas, he never returned. I had, I think, a rather deprived childhood sexually, although I was only vaguely aware of it at the time. Things were to change after I entered Harvard College. Not that my sexual life became more satisfying; alas no, the change was in my perception of my deprivation.

In July 1849 I entered Harvard College as a Freshman. I was fifteen, a bit younger than most of my classmates, but since Father was a professor, the other boys did not question my being there.[1] I continued to live at home, however, and so enjoyed little of the sense of adventure that my classmates who lived on campus felt. I later regretted this and begged Father to allow me to live on campus, something he agreed to only in my Senior year, which I spent in Massachusetts Hall.

The Great Event of my first year as a Harvard student was the grisly murder of Dr. Parkman by Dr. Webster. Even after the jury returned a verdict of guilty my father was still not really convinced of Webster's guilt; not of murder, at any rate; he had already resigned himself to the fact that Webster had indeed killed Parkman.[2] All of the lawyers, and Judge Shaw too, were criticised for the way they

---

[1] Benjamin Peirce (1809–1880) was professor of mathematics at Harvard (1833–1880) and largely responsible for the establishment of the Harvard Observatory. He was also consulting astronomer for the *American Nautical Almanac* (1849–1867).
[2] Numerous accounts of the Parkman/Webster case have been published. One of the more readable and accurate is Helen Thomson, *Murder at Harvard* (Boston: Houghton Mifflin, 1971).

conducted themselves during the trial, and it was generally believed that, even if Webster did kill Parkman, the verdict should not have been murder, but manslaughter.[3] I have wondered whether our discussions about the law during that year may not have influenced my own later decision to study that subject. Of all the books and pamphlets published on the trial, I think I was most impressed by Mr. Spooner's argument. He avoided all discussion of who was telling the truth etc. and concentrated on the simple illegality of the trial, since three prospective jurors had been dismissed because they did not believe in capital punishment. When I began my own study of law, however, I learned that no one took that argument seriously,[4] and, at any rate, I soon discovered that the practice, not to mention the study, of law is seldom as dramatic as the Webster case, and I soon left that subject in disillusion. But I am getting ahead of my story.

It was during my freshman year also that Marshal Tukey of the Boston police initiated those raids he called "descents," which, for example, included wholesale arrests of suspicious persons in bawdy houses. They seemed to have some good effect, but we (I mean, my family and I) were much incensed that innocent people were exposed to injustices. The matter became much worse shortly after when Tukey started his weekly practice of what he called his "show-up of rogues." Here, he simply rounded up any group of people he found unpleasant and exposed them to public ridicule, forcing them to run a gauntlet of the gathered mob, who shouted and spit and threw rocks at them, sometimes reaching out and tearing their clothing. They (the mob, I mean) were the real criminals, I felt. The most pitiable case was a young woman who was in the habit of dressing as a man. The mob

[3] The legal aspect of the trial of Dr. Webster has been carefully investigated in Robert Sullivan, *The Disappearance of Dr. Parkman* (Boston: Little, Brown and Company, 1971).
[4] Lysander Spooner, *Illegality of the Trial of John W. Webster* (Boston: Bela Marsh, 1850), 16 pp. Spooner's argument has received more attention in recent years.

tore off nearly all her clothes, and in the process tore her flesh, too, so that the poor woman was bloody and covered with the filth that had been thrown at her before she could get away. She was never accused of any real crimes, but the fact that she was "different" was crime enough in the eyes of most people. I have often wondered what became of her; of course I never saw her, I only read about the incident in the newspapers. The mob acted at that time in such a repulsive way that some people became courageous enough to speak out against Tukey's tactics, and indeed he did tone them down somewhat afterwards.

It never occurred to me then to connect the woman's act of dressing as a man with my own sexual feelings, which I was gradually perceiving as also somehow "different." But this difference I saw at the time as something entirely peculiar to me.

I should note here that my excitement over the murder of Dr. Parkman did not prevent my enjoyment of the stage, particularly Shakespeare, which was already a growing passion. In a letter I wrote to a cousin about the murder I also said: "I went to see Miss Cush man as Lady Macbeth, Wednesday. She is a splendid actress, but miserably supported." I saw Charlotte Cushman several times, and I think it was she who really propelled my interest in Shakespeare. I know I copied some of her facial expressions in my own dramatic readings. I thought her "splendid" not only in the role of Lady Macbeth, but also in male roles, which her vigorous and fiery temperament enabled her to play with much success. I greatly enjoyed her Hamlet, and I think I fell in love with her as Romeo. Many women also fell in love with her, including three American sculptresses, I believe, and an English writer who made her the model of the heroine in a rather scandalous novel.[5]

---

[5] A Boston native, Charlotte Cushman (1816–1876) appeared at the Tremont Theatre in 1835 as Countess Almaviva in *The Marriage of Figaro*, but her singing voice failing her she entered the drama, and played Lady Macbeth in the same year. She was on the stage until 1858, in American and in London. In her later years she was much appreciated as a dramatic reader. Jonathan Ned

By my Junior year I had become thick friends with my classmates Rantoul and Shaw, and took a more active part in college life. Of course we called ourselves the "Three Musketeers"; the Dumas novel had been published only a few years earlier, but was immediately translated into English, and we had devoured it. Shaw and I were close, but Rantoul was our leader, and I think we were both in love with him; I know I was. In the summer after my Sophomore year Shaw, who lived in Boston, and I went to Beverly for an overnight visit with Rantoul.

How vivid that visit remains even today! It was the first time that Rantoul and I were intimate, and although there was no real sexual contact between us, I recall that first visit as more satisfying even than my later visits with him. The three of us slept in one room in two beds, Shaw in one while I shared the other with Rantoul. We stayed awake late that night, too excited to sleep. I was burning to touch my companion, but did not dare. When my hand nevertheless brushed him (by chance?) he matter-of-factly took it in both of his and held it firmly on his chest as he calmly continued the conversation. The room was faintly lit by the moon, but Shaw could not see that Rantoul was holding my hand, since all but our heads were under the covers. I was in ecstasy and did not dare speak or even move. Rantoul, however, held my hand as if it were the most natural thing in the world and answered Shaw's questions in his usual calm and confident manner. He was telling us of his personal philosophy, a sort of conscious egoism (for he insisted that all men are really egoists and that it is their unawareness of this which makes them evil). Later I came to better understand and appreciate his insights; at the moment, however, I was

---

Katz wrote that Cushman's life "involved a series of intimate relations with other women" and he listed several of them in his *Gay American History: Lesbians and Gay Men in the U.S.A.* (New York: Thomas Y. Crowell, 1976), p. 654.

unable to concentrate on his words, for I was completely absorbed by the feeling of well-being that flowed through me. I felt protected from all the hurtful forces in the world in that instant. I worshipped him. It never occurred to me to ask what he felt for me; he accepted me and that was all that mattered to me then. Later I demanded more; but not then, and that was what made the moment complete. The nearest I came later to that peculiar feeling was with Tom. But by then my need for "protection" was not as great and at any rate my relationship with Tom was far more complex from the beginning.

I believe it was this year, or possibly the next, that the three of us went to see the famous experiment of the pendulum hung inside of the Bunker Hill Monument from the top, to demonstrate the rotation of the earth. That the earth did rotate was, of course, an accepted fact soon after its suggestion by Copernicus, but its experimental proof came surprisingly late. That was in 1851, when Foucault performed his celebrated pendulum experiment at the Pantheon in Paris. When this was reported, there was a rush throughout the world to construct similar pendulums. The one at the Bunker Hill Monument was all the rage at the time, but I think we were among the last to see it.[6]

In my Junior year I won the Bowdoin Prize for my English dissertation "The past and future history of the English language in America." Horatio Alger, Jr., won the Senior Prize. I did not know him well, but rather liked him. Of course I knew nothing at the time of his interest in boys.[7]

The most exciting event of that year was my escape from the Hudson River steamship "Henry Clay," which burned on July 28,

---

[6] Jean Bernard Léon Foucault (1819–1868). Foucault's pendulum was about 200 feet long. The Bunker Hill Monument was built in 1843 of Quincy granite, in the form of an obelisk 221 feet high.
[7] Horatio Alger (1832–1899) writer of more than 100 enormously popular books for boys, including *Ragged Dick* (1867) and other series. On Alger's pederastic interests, see Edwin P. Hoyt, *Horatio's Boys: The Life and Work of Horatio Alger, Jr.* (Radnor, PA: Chilton, 1974).

1852, shortly before it reached New York on its trip from Albany. At the time I did not realise the extent of the catastrophe—only enough to know that my parents would worry about me, so I sent them a telegram as soon as I could to let them know that I was safe.[8]

The most important event of my Senior year was my move from home to Massachusetts Hall. I had wanted to do this earlier and begged Father to allow it. He had been reluctant, partly because of the added expense, but my youngest brother Bertie was now three years old and five children in the house, in addition to the servants that such a household required, began to crowd him, and so he finally agreed. I continued to see my family often, of course, but the move was liberating for me in ways I did not foresee. I was able to see my friends much more than before, since they were now able to "drop in" at any time. The new privacy also allowed, or perhaps promoted, experiments in sexuality. Shaw and I became intimate, though with us the intimacy was more talk than anything else. We hugged one another and laughed uncontrollably over our private jokes. Our favorite invention was an explanation of the name "Hasty Pudding" for the Harvard "dramatic club," which we joined that year. We insisted that the name was a disguise for the real name, which was "Premature Ejaculators." It took only an exchange of "H.P.?"—"P.E.!" to send us into gales of laughter.[9]

In fact, we much enjoyed our participation in the club. I was in no less than five productions that year. Most of my parts were simply great fun, but that of Letitia Ogle in "Matrimonial Difficulties" was a bit of an adventure. I liked the fact that only boys were in our

---

[8] The fire on the *Henry Clay* apparently resulted from an overheating of the boilers during a race between it and the steamship *Armenia*. Among the dozens of lives that were lost was Nathaniel Hawthorne's younger sister Maria Louise.

[9] When twenty-one Harvard students formed a social club in 1795, they mandated that "the members in alphabetical order shall provide a pot of hasty pudding for every meeting." Hence the name Hasty Pudding for the club. The theatrical tradition began in 1844 and has continued since.

productions, but I did not like playing the part of a girl. The boy who did so was made fun of by the other boys; but since girls were simply not available, somebody had to do it. Even though, as I now realise, I was always more attracted to boys and men sex ually than to girls and women, I have never felt particularly feminine myself. Ulrichs's theory in this matter has lately been revived in Germany and has also gained some acceptance here, but, as I wrote Symonds, I cannot agree with it. Still, I must have had ambig uous feelings in the matter at the time. At any rate, the male lead in "Matrimonial Difficulties" was a boy I had long admired from a distance and thought unapproachable. He was very handsome, athletic, in the bloom of health, had a charming personality, and—as would be expected—was liked by all. Naturally he appeared to me to be far more mature than he probably really was; this view was also helped by the rumors of his various sexual escapades with girls in Boston. Thus it is no wonder that I had twice the difficulty remembering my lines for that production!

The first time we practiced the "reconciliation scene" in which he put his arms around me, I got an erection. This was embarrassing for me, since we were not yet practicing in costume and so it could be noticed. In fact, I think no one did notice, but I was always afraid it would happen again, and this fear did not let me fully enjoy the scene or indeed to play the part with conviction. Nevertheless, I was able to relax a few times with him and enjoy the sexual energy that he exuded. I do not know if this was noticed by him. Since probably most people, male and female, reacted in some way to his energy, it was simply the world that he lived in; he accepted it—and took from it what he wanted. In this case, it was clear that he did not want *me*, but that did not stop his enjoyment of his own part, his enjoyment of himself, so to speak.

The experience caused me to give a great deal of thought to my own sexuality, which began to impress me more and more as— what shall I say?—as different. But different from what? Already as a Freshman it was clear that the interest in girls that my classmates expressed was not mine. At first I attributed this to the fact that they were all some what older than I; thus I kept silent and expected to share their interests soon. This did not happen, however, and I began to think that it was all talk, or at any rate that they tended to exaggerate their interest. It was, after all, conventional and expected. It was years before I could accept as fact their strongly felt sexual interest in girls, and even then this acceptance was only intellectual, almost one of the will. Deep down I have never *felt* convinced of it.

It was about then that I had my first really sexual dream. It is still vivid in my memory: The body of a beautiful, nude man, young, golden, gleaming with sweat, is on a bed. I lie on top of him with my face in the angle of his right shoulder and neck. A feeling of exaltation floods over me. And yet, I feel that the situation is somehow incomplete. Still, I do not know what is to come next. Suddenly he slides me down his body until my face is directly over his penis. I immediately take it into my mouth. It is surprisingly small, too small, but with a stiff hard core . . . Alas, the dream ended there and I awoke with my heart pounding. Such an act seemed impossible to me at that time and I told the dream to no one. Little did I suspect that I would enjoy many such acts—starting in the not very distant future.

At age eighteen my sexual ideas were still confused but, at any rate, did not prevent my greatly enjoying my Senior year. It was also during this year that my interest, not simply in the stage, but in the musical stage developed. Opera has since been a passion with me. I have had the pleasure of seeing more than once the greatest actor

(Coquelin) and the greatest singer (Eames) of our time. And though I cannot sing at all, I more than once had the pleasure of sharing the Boston operatic stage as a supernumerary.

With all these activities, the wonder is that I did as well in my studies as I did. In particular, I discovered that I had genuine ability in mathematics; but since I was the son of the mathematics professor, no one was surprised by this, and I too accepted it as only natural. My interest in the subject was genuine and I used it to write an English oration for commencement that won me my second Bowdoin Prize, this time as a Senior: "The Relation of Mathematics to Modern Science." It contained much bombast and little originality, but was probably sincere enough and just the thing people like to hear.

The oration ended in a really dreadful expression of piety that was, however, mostly conventional, for if I had no doubts about my religion then, neither did I have strong feelings. These came later, along with the feelings of guilt over my sexuality. But more of that later. At any rate, it was neither religion nor mathematics that I chose at that time for my   future career, but law. In fact, I was more attracted to mathematics, but felt overshadowed by Father's ability. The apparent reason for my choice, however, was the fact that both Shaw and Rantoul had already decided in favour of law.[10] Rantoul did not immediately attend a law school, but worked in a law office in Boston for the next year. Unlike me, Shaw was unconcerned about being overshadowed by his father (who was, after all, Chief Justice of the Supreme Court of Massachusetts and had presided over the trial of Dr. Webster). Thus Shaw and I entered the Harvard Law School together in the fall of 1853.

---

[10] Samuel Savage Shaw had a successful legal career. Robert Samuel Rantoul early entered party politics and held several elective and appointive offices. Shaw never married; Rantoul did and had nine children.

THREE
LAW AND DIVINITY

SINCE RANTOUL CAME in from Beverly every day to his Boston office, I also saw him rather regularly, and we (he, Shaw, and I) continued our practice of "monthlies," when we all gathered in turn in one another's rooms. And rather than return to his home in Beverly, Rantoul sometimes stayed overnight. Those were glorious times for me, for my feeling for him ran deep. Our friendship had also been promoted by the accident of our names being close in alphabetical order, which meant that we were never separated in the classroom by more than two classmates; and in the last year, when the variety of subjects made for smaller groups so that Peterson and Pome roy were not always with us, we often sat side by side. By now I was no longer content to simply hold hands; nor did my advances meet any resistance from him. He seemed so solid, so secure—and I felt so safe in his arms. And although he did not return the passion I felt for him, our relationship was not entirely one-sided. I think that what he felt for me was more a tenderness than anything else. When I tried to tell him how I felt and stumbled for words, he would hold me close, say "I know, I know," and kiss me on the forehead or, sometimes, on the mouth. And I would relax, total contentment, in his arms. Naturally those sessions were not with out animal enjoyment of sex, for we were at the height of our sexual energy. Indeed, my own excitement was such that I often had an orgasm before I realised it was about to hap pen. With Rantoul it was different; some direct action was required, and it was a service I gladly performed. My reward was in sensing his satisfaction and the embrace of gratitude that invariably followed. Only with Tom later did I experience such bliss. With Tom I was more aware of myself and my feelings could consequently be deeper, but my experiences with Rantoul were a unique absorption in the moment and I have never lost the memory of the warm feelings I had for him.

I remember in particular the "monthly" when we met in Shaw's room in late November 1853. Shaw had wanted to have Rantoul sleep overnight with him, but I gave him all kinds of reasons why Rantoul should stay with me, and he finally gave in. We enjoyed the evening together, catching up on all our own news and that of our former classmates. Shaw, who was perhaps a bit jealous, let fall a couple of allusions to let us know that he knew why I insisted that Rantoul come with me, but nothing spoiled the evening. Back in my room, I was, as usual, a bit nervous, though I tried to hide it. He, as always, seemed to have nothing to hide and appeared as relaxed as ever. (I was to learn later that Rantoul was a far more complicated person than I had thought.) I offered him a nightcap, but it was already two o'clock and he not unexpectedly declined it, saying that he was tired and wished to go to bed directly. His smile, when he said this, showed not the slightest trace of fatigue. This circumstance naturally heightened my excitement, for I was looking forward to lying in the arms of an awake Rantoul. He must have seen me tremble; he smiled again, came closer, wrapped his arms around me, and said, "It's all right." Indeed, all was right in my world. That night he even seemed to want me, want me as much as I wanted him. We talked even less than usual. I was afraid to break the spell; he obviously did not wish—or perhaps was unable—to reveal to me the thoughts that were going through his mind. At any rate, I must have satisfied some deep-felt, if temporary, need, for his display of tenderness and affection was greater than ever before. He genuinely gave himself to me.   It was an overwhelming experience; nothing I have felt since then compares with it—not even with Tom. (Damn these eternal comparisons with Tom!) Perhaps it was because it was the experience, not the person, that impressed itself on me. With Tom it was always—well, uniquely Tom.

Alas, that experience was not repeated. I continued to see Rantoul, but he never again reacted to my interest in quite the same way. I searched myself for the cause, but quickly realised that, whatever it was, it was beyond my control, and my feeling for him gradually relaxed its hold on me. This was helped by another and very unexpected development: my youthful idealism had begun to turn to religion for its fulfillment. The eventual result was my determination to become a Unitarian minister. That decision did not come for several more years, however. A more immediate literary result was my essay "The character and philosophy of Malebranche," which won me my third Bowdoin Prize, this time as a Resident Graduate. I now find the exalted religious tone on which that essay ends painful, but I suppose it was a sincere expression of my feelings.

In the meantime, I dropped my study of law after only one year—in which I was never very interested—and fell back on mathematics, where I felt on much safer ground. In the summer of 1854 Eliot and I were appointed tutors in mathematics.[1] I have often thought that it

---

[1] Charles W. Eliot (1834–1926) was Peirce's classmate. President of Harvard for forty years (1869–1909), he promoted the plan of embracing all undergraduate studies in Harvard College and

was this early collaboration that made our later efforts to develop the Graduate School so smooth and enjoyable—and successful. Eliot had a forceful personality and there is no question that he was the leader; I cannot help but think, however, that in many ways I contributed equally to all that we achieved. And from the beginning we were innovative, for we introduced the first written examinations in Harvard College.[2] The experiment was so successful that it was immediately adopted by other departments and was soon the accepted practice.

We remained tutors for four years, longer than either of us expected. I also stayed much longer than I expected in my new rooms in Massachusetts Hall, to which I moved in May 1854, for I did not move again for ten years. Although the space was larger, I did not have a permanent second bed until I moved to Holworthy Hall in 1864. This did not prevent my having overnight visitors, for we were young enough not to mind "roughing it" a bit. But the sexual encounters became less and less frequent as they were burdened with more and more guilt. This must have resulted from several factors: there was, first of all, my youthful idealism, a sort of "I was born for greater things" attitude. Then too, I was no longer of an age when I could dismiss my actions as "juvenile experiments." I had to face up to the fact that my chums were genuinely more interested in girls, were indeed becoming married. Of course marriage seemed to me, too, to be the ideal state; and if I could not achieve it, rather than fall below it, I determined to rise above it. If I could not stop loving men—and I did not want to stop—then it should be for more "honorable" motives, and not because I wanted to touch them. Thus I struggled to elevate my thoughts.

gathering about it a complete group of graduate and professional schools.
[2] For the early collaboration between Peirce and Eliot, see Hubert Kennedy, "The first written examinations at Harvard College," *The American Mathematical Monthly* 87 (1980): 483–486.

Needless to say, I often fell. Sometimes my companion felt as guilty as I did. More often, he took it lightly—and then I tried to convince him of his guilt. The unavoidable result was that such friendships tended to be of very short duration. I knew the Biblical references to Sodom and Gomorrah, of course, and began to feel weak indeed for giving in to such feelings. During my hours in the law library I also searched the case books for crimes that are described in our laws in just such Biblical terms. Oddly, it seemed that the early colonists were more often prosecuted for having sexual intercourse with turkeys than with other men. The law itself made little distinction between their actions and mine. Although I had earlier thought that I was prompted by love or at least affection, I now tried to see my acts as coming from a basically evil nature. I read again and again the story of the fall of Adam and Eve, and began to see myself as a fallen creature who must call on his Creator for redemption. I adopted a practice of regular prayer and meditation. I remained friendly with Shaw, but my former levity began to give way to an 'elevated' tone. In short, I was on the way to becoming a religious fanatic.

This did not prevent my continued enjoyment of the stage and opera in particular. Giuseppe Mario and Giulia Grisi were on tour in the U. S. in 1854, and Shaw and I eagerly awaited their arrival in Boston in the winter, when we spent several nights in the upper gallery of the theatre.[3] The general enthusiasm for their performances of Italian opera became, in Shaw's word, an "epidemic." Though I admired Grisi, I was taken with Mario and still think him the greatest tenor I have heard. His voice had a rich velvet quality that has been unsurpassed. No doubt I was also influenced by his handsome face and graceful figure, which, despite his age, had the charm of youth.

---

[3] Giuseppe Mario, born Giovanni Count of Candia (1810–1883), was the most famous tenor of the 19th century. Giulia Grisi (1811–1869) divorced her first husband and married Mario in 1856.

My tutoring in mathematics took a great deal of time and effort, but was very rewarding. I think the boys appreciated my patience with them; and I gradually began to develop my own ways of presenting the various subjects. I saw that Father's book in analytic geometry, for example, contained brilliant insights, which I could appreciate, but was on the whole not entirely suited to younger minds—or, I should say, to beginners in the subject. I discussed the matter with Eliot, who urged me to attempt a revision. I hesitated for a long while before approaching Father with the idea; it seemed very presumptuous of me to suppose that I could improve on his book, which was, after all, the recognised standard work. But when I did get the courage to talk with him about it, he surprised me by immediately agreeing to a revision. He even suggested that I write my own book and substitute it in the course for his. I did not have the courage for that! But the final result, which was published in 1857, while continuing to have Father's name on the title page ("on the Basis of Professor Peirce's Treatise"), was in fact very much my work. The students continued to grumble at having to study such matters, but in fact the performance of the first class to use the book was a noticeable improvement over that of the earlier classes. That was gratifying; but my greatest satisfaction came from Father's praise, for he genuinely seemed to appreciate my effort— though, as far as I could tell, he never adopted any of my innovations in his own courses.

In the meantime, Shaw had competed his studies in the Harvard Law School and, after another year in a Boston law office, had been admitted to the Bar in April 1856. He short ly after left for nearly a year and a half in Europe, the first of numerous such trips he was to make. His successful pursuit of his chosen career made me all the more aware of my own indecision.

Cambridge, April 22, 1856

Dear Shaw,

I called at the club on Saturday afternoon without finding you. So I write to bid you good-bye and to beg you to write to me as often as you can. Mortals do not know what you will find me at when you return, whether Law or Divinity or neither. I don't know but I shall spend my time in reading Novalis as I have been looking this morning into the volume you returned with such delight, especially at what he says about Mathematics.

I finally decided in favour of Divinity, entering the Harvard Divinity School in March 1857. I was busy indeed, for I continued to be a tutor for another year; my desire to be financially independent made this necessary, and an increase in salary in September helped me realise it. To my surprise, Horatio Alger also returned to the Divinity School (after being there briefly in the fall of 1853). I spoke with him a few times, but we were never close. At any rate, I did not have time for him, for my course kept me too busy. He must have been otherwise occupied as well, for his graduation came a year after mine, which was in 1859. My studies were helped by an exchange I made with my old classmate Edward Pearce of Providence, Rhode Island. Pearce, who had been a better mathematics student than I, was at the time a proctor at Harvard, but had long wanted to try teaching. He readily agreed to my suggestion that we exchange positions, and we jointly submitted our proposal to the Overseers for their approval. We kept our new positions for three years, something I believe neither of us expected. I'm sure I did not; for I expected I would be settled as a Unitarian minister before then.

In 1859 my family celebrated a double graduation: my brother Charles from Harvard College, and I from the Divinity School, at whose commencement I delivered a paper on "Science and the Supernatural," still trying to reconcile the two. And I continued to do so in several of my subsequent sermons. Those sermons were, in fact, well received, but cost me great efforts to prepare—and then were never praised for the ideas that seemed most important to me, but, as it seemed to me, for the occasions when I lapsed into conventional banality. I discussed some of this with Father, who was appropriately sympathetic, but of little real help. Although conventionally pious, he felt that "serving science" was "serving God," and stated his faith in my mathematical abilities. I was grateful for that and for his offer to help me obtain a mathematical position somewhere, should I decide not to pursue the ministry, but I was determined to give my best effort to becoming a minister and would not allow myself to consider another alternative so long as I had a chance of succeeding.

Sincerity can often be painful, and the following two years had more than their share. I dare say little of this showed to others. Well-wishers assured me that I would soon be "settled," as the Unitarians say, but that day never seemed to come, although I "praught" in various churches with a good degree of acceptance. (Friends assured me that the prop er past tense of "preach" is "preached," but on the analogy of "teach, taught," which all admitted, I continued to say "preach, praught," an idiosyncrasy that caused people to laugh behind my back, but which I stubbornly kept.) One of the earliest occasions was in Salem in October 1859. Rantoul came to that Sunday's service with his wife, the former Harriet Neal of Salem, whom he had married the year before. He had also moved to Salem at that time. I had met Mrs. Rantoul in 1853, shortly before their engagement. She was not yet seventeen at the time and still a school girl. This no doubt explained part of their long engagement. Rantoul slyly suggested that I, too, should marry, but what he really thought in the matter, I do not know. They already had one child and it appeared to me that another was on the way. They eventually had nine children and I saw several of the boys later as students at Harvard. In view of families like this in Massachusetts I did not feel that the Biblical injunction to "go forth and multiply" applied to me personally.

The following Sunday I praught in Boston and few weeks later in Medford. In January (1860) I even praught in King's Chapel in Boston, the same sermon as in Salem, but it caused quite a stir the second time.

[The following is from Peirce's letter-book.]

Cambridge, January 16, 1860
Dear Rantoul,

I have had it in my heart to write to you ever since my last visit at Salem; but have not hitherto on account of having my hands full of other matters. But I now wish to say that I am on the eve of a journey south which will probably last during the college vacation. I go first to Charleston, S.C., where I am engaged to preach three Sundays, then on a visit of a few day to Columbia, S.C., and on my way home I expect to stop at Washington, Baltimore, Philadelphia, and New York. I do not preach at Charleston as a candidate, but only in a sort of preliminary way, in fact just as I preach anywhere. I leave possibly tomorrow P.M. but I fear I shall hardly get off before the next morning. Since I was in Salem, I have praught at Quincy, two Sundays at King's Chapel, and yesterday morning at Dr. Dewey's, i.e., Judge Shaw's. I am quite pleased to have this coming variety in my labours and in every way I expect to enjoy my visit at Charleston very much. I wish you would write to me there. Address me at the Mills House. I shall be there until the 5th of February.

I understand that one of my sermons at the King's Chapel made some discussion at the time and shocked the conservative prejudices of a number of people. It was the one what I gave at Mr. Clapp's church on "Jesus Christ the same yesterday, today, and tomorrow." Perhaps you will have some remembrance of it. I have received a note from old Dr. Jackson full of very warm commendation of it, and I find that many of those who heard me are of the same way of feeling as he. Still I cannot help being aware that my views are in some respects less orthodox than the body of the attendants in Unitarian churches. And tho' I am not disposed to press them, still many feel in all my preaching, whatever subject I select, the *absence* of some arguments and sanctions which seem to them important. I am glad I have you and Mrs. Rantoul to so great an extent for sympathisers and parishioners. I cannot help thinking that it would be a better way if the preacher and not the congregation made the church; i.e., if the preacher undertook to preach and was free to gather to himself all that would come and felt themselves benefited by him, and if contrary minded would go another way. This however is theoretical.

In Charleston I was treated very kindly and I believe my sermons were well received. Although I had told Rantoul that I was not a candidate there, this was, in fact, an informal understanding and I considered it such. I had hoped they would make a decision while I was there, but that did not happen and I returned to Cambridge to await word from them. When it finally came, it was a "we regret to inform you"—and I breathed a tremendous sigh of relief. I felt that a great burden had been lifted from me. I realised that I did not want to be settled there. Although I had been well treated personally, I was shocked by what I saw as monstrous hypocrisy on the part of the Charleston congregation—a well-established one, having been founded in 1777. The Church taught the "brotherhood of man," and yet one saw slaves everywhere, with nothing ever said against the institution. Human beings were sold just as if they were mere tables and chairs, while others lived from their labour. I cannot say that the relatively few Negroes in Boston were—or are, for that matter—well treated; but the difference was enormous and I felt it strongly. I never returned to the South—not south of Washington, at any rate.

I have always felt the force of human injustice. I have felt it against me for being "different," even though my life has been relatively easy. I have tried, in my own small way, to treat others, if not equally, at least with equal dignity. I have tried to act with personal courtesy. But how can one be courteous to a "slave"? No, nothing makes up for a loss of liberty.

Discouraged by not becoming settled, I began to question whether I really was "called" to the pulpit. This may not have been perceived by those around me. My brother Charles, at any rate, wrote me from one of his expeditions to Bird Island on April 4:

> I haven't heard that you have any particular desire to be settled at present, which I am not greatly surprised at, good sermons not being writable off hand & I suppose nothing could be pleasanter than living in Cambridge & being able to give as much attention as ever you wish to what you are engaged on.
>
> I wrote a note of thanks to Waters for his trouble & represented that life was of little value unless you made some advance in the family genealogy.

This last comment cut me terribly at the time, since I did not expect to make an "advance in the family genealogy," but I tried to dismiss it as simply typical of Charles' lack of sensitivity to my feelings. Looking back now, I see only the irony in the situation, for Charles himself made no "advance in   the family genealogy" even with his two marriages.[4] He was right on one thing, however; life in Cambridge was pleasant. Shortly after his letter I was again appointed tutor in mathematics, Father having requested a short leave of absence, and I continued in that position through the summer; in the fall I became "Class Tutor of the Freshman Class." And of course I was still a proctor, so I was busy enough and, in fact, praught only sporadically.

[4] Charles Sanders Peirce (1839–1914) married Harriet Melusina Fay in 1862; he was divorced from her in 1883, when he married Juliette Froissy. A physicist, mathematician, and logician, C. S. Peirce is considered by some to be the most original thinker and greatest logician of his time. There is a Charles S. Peirce Society, which actively promotes interest in his ideas and writings.

It was during this time that I learned that some of the students had fastened on me the name "Squirty," due to my supposed superior scholarship. (In those days a good recitation was termed a "squirt" at Harvard.) Happily, that name did not stay with me.

By the following spring (1861) it seemed to me that I must come to some kind of decision in the matter of the ministry. Just then I heard of an opening in a Unitarian church at Staten Island. I applied for the position, was invited to visit, and spent a couple of weeks there, preaching several times and meeting all the pillars of that church. But in the end nothing came of it.

Or rather, much came of it. For with the end of any real prospect of settlement, I realised that what I really wanted all along was to stay on at Harvard. Once again I discussed the matter with Father. He seemed not at all surprised; I think he must have expected it. More important, he had a suggestion that, if successful, would relieve me of the tutor-proctor routine and at the same time improve my financial situation. His confidence did not immediately relieve my anxiety, but in fact he was successful and a permanent career at Harvard soon seemed assured.

FOUR
MATHEMATICIAN IN LOVE

AFTER OUR FOUR years as Tutors in Mathematics, Eliot had accepted the position of Assistant Professor of Chemistry and Mathematics. By now this had become a burden to him and it turned out that he was willing to give up the mathematics half of his position. Father learned of this and asked me if I should like to take over his mathematical duties. I thought it strange that he was so willing to have me leave my profession of the ministry, but it seemed to me a perfect opportunity to do so and at the same time take a step toward permanent financial independence. At Father's suggestion I wrote to President Felton on August 15, 1861:

> My dear Sir,
>
> I am now prepared to say that I will accept the assistant-professorship of Mathematics if the offer of it still stands open. I learn, however, from my Father that it is doubtful whether the corporation will be able to continue to support that place. If they should find themselves unable to do so, I fear I should have

to relinquish the idea of returning to college work. I should hardly feel that I was justified in taking a tutorship at a salary of eight hundred dollars. I can have no sanguine hope that expenses now cut off by the pressure of the times can be soon resumed, and it seems to me I ought not to change my previous plans of life for an uncertainty or to try a temporary experiment.

I think my Father sufficiently understands my views, if you are disposed to ask any further questions.

Yours with much respect and regard,

J. M. Peirce

As it turned out, my fears that the Corporation would simply try to have my services at the lower salary of tutor were exaggerated and at their meeting at the end of the summer the Corporation duly elected me Assistant Professor of Mathematics. Even then I was kept waiting for over two years before the Overseers confirmed my election.

The amount of committee work in my new position seemed enormous to me. There was some variety in the assignments, but I seemed to be a near-permanent fixture of the Tabular View committee, to which I was first appointed in the summer of 1862. In fact, I believe I brought a real improvement to the method of arranging and displaying the courses so as to make them understandable to the Freshmen particularly. Tom, who entered Harvard College that year, later told me that he was much impressed with my explanation of the Tabular View. In fact, he ever after associated me with it, jokingly referring to me as the King of the Tabular View.

Tom (I must once give his full name: Thomas Sergeant Perry)[1]

[1] Thomas Sergeant Perry (1845–1928), author, scholar, and educator, was born at Newport, R. I. He was the grandson of Oliver Hazard Perry, of Lake Eire fame, whose brother, Commodore Matthew

was in the logic class I taught in his first semester. I noticed him at once; he had the kind of charm that immediately attracted. He was extraordinarily handsome, with an engaging smile, the type which seems to be very much alive and to enjoy being alive. I was quite taken by him and caught myself stealing glances at him. I tried to be even-handed with the class, however, and thought that he did not see my special interest in him. But Tom understood me even then; we were discussing this only a couple of years ago and he gave me a copy of a letter he wrote to his brother-in-law John La Farge[2] in February 1863:

I hope Jimmie Peirce will not get too much glow in him about *me*; he will be greatly disappointed next term when he gets me in mathematics. He is an exceedingly unpopular man, although I think from my little knowledge of him, he is unjustly so. He heard us in Logic for 4 months last term, during which time, with two recitations a week and some of them deads, almost all slumps, I never saw him lose his temper. He was always equally calm if we made a very good or a very bad recitation. But he is very hard in mathematics, the sophomores tell me. What did you think of him? He is somewhat famous as a reader of Shakespeare, a clergyman and as a mathematician in this quarter.

How perceptive Tom was even then! And, despite all his problems with mathematics—for he really was a mathematical disaster—I am happy to know that he never lost his good opinion of me.

This was also the year that I was drafted for the War. Since the apportionment for Cambridge was made on the basis which includes college students, there were a high number drafted. Indeed, of the eight officers of the college faculty who were liable, four of us were

Cal braith Perry, became equally famous because of his negotiations with Japan. On his mother's side, Perry was a direct descendant of Benjamin Franklin. When he entered Harvard College—when Peirce first saw him—he was sixteen years old. For an excellent life of Perry, see Virginia Harlow, *Thomas Sergeant Perry: A Biography* (Durham, NC: Duke University Press, 195).
[2] John La Farge (1835–1910), American artist, chiefly of landscapes.

selected in July 1863, along with a large number of students. I had expected this for some time and had also discussed the possibility with Father. We had decided that every effort would be made to keep me in Cambridge. Father himself was not unsympathetic to the South, having many friends there from among his former students. Nor did he feel the moral outrage against the institution of slavery that I did. But I, too, was convinced that the actual causes of the War had far less to do with slavery than the abolitionists wanted us to believe. Thus Father immediately intervened, arguing that my services at Harvard College were essential and arranging to buy a replacement. I, of course, could not have afforded this, but he had put a sum aside precisely for this contingency. The result was, therefore, that I was able to continue teaching my usual courses. The other teacher of mathematics, tutor Solomon Lincoln, was also drafted, but, as he had already resigned at the end of the college year, his absence was anticipated. He was replaced by F. G. Bromberg, who stayed with us until the end of the War.

This did not mean, of course, that we did not feel the tragedy of the War. I especially felt it with the death of Charles Russell Lowell in October 1864. Charles was less than a year younger than I, and I was quite fond of him, as indeed I was of the whole family. I had spent many a delightful evening in their home, taking part in the mutual entertainment. My specialty was Shakespeare recitations; my gestures were often thought odd, but on the whole my performances were genuinely appreciated. Because of my closeness to the family, they asked me to write the article about him that was published in 1866 in the two-volume *Harvard Memorial Biographies* of Harvard alumni who died in the War. It was a painful duty, made easy, however, by the gratitude of the family and their cooperation in furnishing all necessary information.

The terrible years of the War finally came to an end in 1865. An event of note closer to home that year was the graduation from Harvard College of my brother Benjamin Mills[3] (like me, named after our maternal grandfather Mills); he left for Paris in the fall to attend the Ecole des Mines for two years. Also in 1865, Eliot was appointed Professor of Chemistry in the newly founded Massachusetts Institute of Technology. My own situation also improved considerably after Father interceded with President Hill to raise my salary. In typical fashion he posed the matter as a vote of confidence in my ability. I later learned (when Eliot pointed out to me Father's letter in the President's file) that he was willing to have my increase deducted from his own salary! Happily, this was not done—and was, no doubt, not really expected by Father—and the increase was duly approved. I appreciated Father's action at the time and even more so after I read his letter, which included the lines: "My Dear President, the time seems to me to have come, when it is proper for me to urge upon the corporation an increase of salary of the assistant professor in my department. . . . In the discharge of his duties, unless I am very much blinded by paternal affection, he has manifested an extraordinary ability, real and potential, so that I think he has earned the right to this manifestation of confidence."

The following year (1866) marked a turning point in my life in ways that I did not expect. I had long wanted to go to Europe and my desire was made all the stronger by Ben's departure the year before; his letters from Paris showed that he was enjoying a delightful life as a student there. Thus, after arranging that G. S. Pierce[4] be appointed

---

[3] Benjamin Mills Peirce (1844–1870). After graduating from the Ecole des Mines, Paris, he briefly studied at the University of Freiburg (Germany). In 1867–1868 he worked in Iceland and Green land, and wrote the U.S. Government report on mineral resources and conditions there. He was a mining engineer in Michigan from 1868 to his death in 1870.
[4] George Winslow Pierce, Harvard Class of 1864, published his own, rather bizarre memoirs: *The Life-Romance of an Algebraist* (Boston: J. G. Cupples, 1891).

tutor in my absence, I was able to take a leave of absence for a year. This was also the year that Tom graduated from Harvard College, and he too left for Europe, staying two years. By then I had spoken to him several times, but I was still shy around him. In fact, Ben was much closer to him, being only a year older; they had become quite good friends as fellow students. Tom went to Paris in November, where he remained for three months, staying in the same hotel with Ben at first, and their friendship became even closer. I had gone to see Ben earlier—my first goal, of course—and was in Germany during most of Tom's visit in Paris, but returned there briefly in January. If I said earlier that I was "taken" by Tom when I first saw him, it was on this occasion that I fell in love.

I had largely gotten over my religious scruples by then, but had continued in the same environment and same narrow way of life. So as to let as little as possible disturb the learning experience that I expected a trip to Europe to be, I determined to try to relax, to be nonjudgmental, to err on the side of acceptance, and to sort things out only after my return to Cambridge. Easier said than done, of course. But the new environment helped, and by the time I returned to Paris I felt more relaxed. It was indeed the case, as Tom said, "What may be a little difficult at home, where jealousy and envy keep one's neigh bors' memory in abnormal activity, becomes very simple abroad." Thus I was able to join Tom and Ben in delightful evenings of wine and talk. This was also a time of "theatrical fervor," as Tom expressed it, when we attended many memorable performances. I have always loved the theatre, and my pleasure was enhanced by Tom's company. Opera has always been my favourite; for this, the highlight of those days was seeing the immortal Adelina Patti. Ironically, however, my most memorable evening followed a quite dismal performance at the Opéra of the opera *Les Indes galantes* of Rameau. Tom and I had gone alone to see it. I thought the performance dull and was easily distracted when I felt Tom's knee pressing against mine. It must have been accidental at first, but when I returned the pressure he must have realised that I wanted it. Typically, Tom pleased me by continuing the contact until the curtain fell.

Afterwards we stopped in a small café for a drink. Tom pressed his ankle against mine and seemed to be testing me to see whether I really wanted the physical contact. I was frightened and excited—and determined to follow his lead. He then suggested a walk through the Tuileries gardens. It was quite cold and the trees were nearly bare; we were almost alone. At one point, hidden from any onlookers by an evergreen, Tom paused and took my hand. I trembled and could not speak. He then placed an arm around my shoulder, drew me closer to him, and placed his lips against mine. As I began to relax, he inserted his tongue—and I melted in his embrace. It was only one kiss, but long and intense, then we hugged one another closely for several moments before we spoke again.

"Tom," I said, "Tom, I . . ."

"Jim," he said, "Jim, you . . ."

And our laughter broke the tension so that we were able to talk. And we did, strolling along the river until we became too cold. I tried to tell him how I felt; my words failed, but he seemed to anticipate what I wanted to say. I was in love and Tom was the object of my love. Tom, too, was in love; but Tom was in love with life. He made me feel, however, that I was a part, an important part of his life. But while my affectional life has centered on Tom ever since, I have remained only one among his many friends and admirers—and, yes, lovers. Yet I never felt rejected by him. Indeed, in recent years, as my sexual urge has diminished, I feel that we have become even closer.

Tom's attraction was more than sexual, but that he had in abundance and it was felt by both sexes. He was also receptive to both. In this he was what I have come to see as the human ideal: the person who has never lost the basic human bisexual condition. Nor was he ever concerned about the difference in our ages. When I expressed by unease over this, he was always able to laugh me out of it.

I changed my travel plans so as to be in Rome later in the spring when Tom planned to be there. Thus I was able to tour that remarkable city in his company. We also went to Naples together. It was on one of our excursions there, as I recall, that Tom let slip, when I was again expressing my concern about the difference in our ages, that this did not help Henry James.[5] They had been childhood chums in Newport, and it seems that Tom knew that James was in love with him; Tom would have welcomed a more intimate friendship with him, but James' nature could never allow him to admit the possibility—not for himself, at any rate.

That was a glorious time for me. I fell in love with the Eternal City and thought I should like to move there when I retired. My feelings for Rome must have been influenced by the glow of seeing it with Tom, however, for when I returned several years later the charm of the city was no longer there for me. Still, the city is fascinating and I would recommend a visit to anyone. But it was Tom I was in love with, and the three times we were able to spend an evening alone together in my room stand out in my memory of Rome. The mere sight of Tom totally naked was overwhelming for me. What beautiful limbs, what smooth

[5] Henry James (1843–1916), the novelist. He was the brother of William James (1842–1910), the psychologist and philosopher, who became Peirce's colleague on the Harvard faculty. Perry was friendly with all the James family; Virginia Harlow's *Thomas Sergeant Perry: A Biography* contains a long appendix of letters to Perry from William, Henry, and Garth Wilkinson James.

skin, how well proportioned, his genitals exactly right . . . I wanted to gaze at him and I wanted to crawl under his skin at the same time. I asked for sexual "favours"; he did not understand. For him it was all so natural; he gave—and got—what he wanted. And I was more than content. After vigorous love-making, spent, I lay in his arms wishing that the moment would last forever, trying to store up the memory, yet knowing it would fade. But knowing, too, that the knowledge of it would sustain me over lonely nights. For I had no illusion that there could be any kind of permanent coupling between us.

The third evening with Tom I did not see him totally naked, but it too was a memorable evening, for this time Tom suggested that we "lie down" before I asked him, as I had the first two times. He also had another surprise for me; he had purchased bright red undershorts in a shop in Rome and wanted to show them off to me, so he did not entirely strip. I admired his purchase, and we laughed; what would our staid New England neigh bors think of such underwear! This time I lay beside him, hugging him closely, and ran my hand over the redness covering his wonderfully formed genitals. I was content with the closeness and Tom's acceptance and genuine affection for me. My love-making progressed no further; anyway, Tom had to leave to keep an appointment with an American acquaintance he had run into during the day. When he dressed to leave, I thanked him for being so good to me, and he gently explained, "I only wanted to show you the red shorts, you could have taken them off." "I will next time," I promised. "There will be a next time, won't there?" "Of course." How could Rome fail to have beautiful memories for me? I glowed for three days in my contentment—while the natives probably thought I only looked smug.

After leaving Tom I returned to Germany, determined to improve my knowledge of the language, which I foresaw would become even more important in mathematics. I wanted to be able to speak it as well as read it, and fortunately the language seemed "comfortable" to me. That is, I could be myself while speaking it, whereas French and Italian, both of which I learned to speak adequately, have always felt foreign to me. I must jolt myself into another personality when I speak them. When I do, I am accepted; but then I feel that I am hypocritical. This never happens in German. (Tom, on the other hand, quickly became fluent in both French and German and claimed to feel equally "at home" in both.) I knew I would soon have to return home; my brother Charles reminded me of what awaited me when he wrote me in July: "Bertie of course has been doing miserably in his studies but his habits are good." (In fact, Bert was able to enter Harvard College, but did not complete his studies, and the fact haunted him for a long while. It is all the more gratifying that he is now having such a successful career in the Foreign Service.)

Charles also wrote: "I have often been to play whist with your friends who must be very fond of you judging from the kind manner toward me." By then I was ready to return. I had been away long enough. I longed to join them in an evening of whist, and I was curious to see what effect my year away in Europe would have on my old life.

In fact, it had little effect on my personal life. I felt that I was more open to sexual overtures, yet none came my way; I felt that I was a greatly changed person, yet no one seemed to notice any difference. True, my status on the faculty seemed slightly elevated, for I had joined the ranks of those who had "done" Europe and this gave me a certain prestige. My knowledge of German also proved valuable. But the majority at Harvard felt the influence of England was more important. To illustrate: the Big Event of the 1867–68 academic year was the arrival in December of Charles Dickens on his American tour. Dickens lost some of his interest for many in Cambridge, however, when he expressed his desire to visit the Medical School "in order to see the exact localities where Professor Webster did that amazing murder and worked so hard to rid himself of the body of the murdered man." After the excitement of the trial and subsequent execution of Dr. Webster, the townspeople soon became very reluctant even to speak of the event.

The liberating effect of my year in Europe also extended to my view of religion. This was reinforced when I learned of an event that occurred during my absence. I still had many acquaintances among the clergy, nearly all of whom seemed eager to inform me (as one of their "own"—the general population was not to know) of the dismissal of Horatio Alger from the First Unitarian Church in Brewster, Massachusetts. After he was initially well received as a minister, it was learned in early 1866 that he had been sexually involved with several boys there. As far as I could learn, this was no more than a bit of fooling around with a few very willing lads of whom Alger was genuinely fond. Yet he was immediately dismissed and every effort was made to hush up the affair for fear of scandal. The expressions of outrage from my former colleagues and their utter condemnation of such actions had a two-fold effect on me: I determined to be very cautious in my own actions, and I formed a very poor opinion of our exemplary clergymen. It is an opinion I continue to hold.

A year after my return from Europe, Tom returned to Harvard to assume a position as tutor of French and German in the fall of 1868. I had greatly looked forward to his return, yet was apprehensive too. Was our intimacy in Rome, I wondered, due to the exotic setting and the fact that we were among strangers? My fears about the difference in our ages also returned. And what would our Harvard colleagues think about a friendship that, from my side at least, might be all too obvious? In fact, my overtures, while not exactly rejected, seemed not to be entirely wanted by him. Not that he was ever unpleasant to me, but there simply seemed to be little time in his life for me. I tried to accept this, but could not help complaining whenever I saw him that it was not often enough and always too brief. His usual answer was: "Jim, I do like you. I'm not trying to avoid you; it's just that I'm busy with all my courses. But wait till next summer. Then we will have lots of time to be together and do things together. Let's tour New England as if it were a Grand Tour of the Continent, shall we?"

Each time I would be cheered up for a short while. But then I grew jealous when I had to see how very close he had become to his classmate Charles Stratton, who was then a lawyer in Boston. In fact, they dined together almost daily. Thus I should have been prepared for what happened in the summer, though I was not—and suffered as a result. For when the time came for the trip I had looked forward to, when I thought I would be alone with Tom in places where no one knew us, where we could renew our intimacy, then came the bombshell: just such a trip was planned with Stratton. I was devastated. I felt alone, abandoned, and with no outlet for my grief—for to whom could I tell my woes? How unfair it all seemed. My brother Ben poured out his troubles to me and expected me to understand his feeling for Kate, whom he could not marry; of course I could not marry Tom, yet I longed to share some of the depth of my feeling for him with Ben. But I knew Ben would not understand, and I dared not, although I could not keep myself from dropping hints in my letters. I suppose I hoped against hope that he would catch a hint and show some sympathy. This never happened, although he must have suspected something. After all, he was close to Tom himself and was together with us in Paris.

After returning from his two years at the Ecole des Mines in Paris, Ben had spent the winter compiling for the U.S. Department of State a report on the condition and resources of Iceland and Greenland. He then took a position in the iron mines near Marquette, Michigan. The weather there did not agree with him and there were other problems, all of which he described to me in a long letter in the spring of 1869, a letter I had great difficulty answering.

> Cambridge, June 12, 1869
> Dear Ben,
>
> I do not know how it has been possible for me to be silent so long, when you have been suffering so much in body and in mind.
>
> As for Kate, of course I am sorry she is coming this way, but I shall bear in mind her kindness to you, and if I can be of service to her, I will gladly render it. You must not, however, exceed the bound of reason in expecting social attentions from Mother and Helen.
>
> I meant to have told you something, a little cheerfuler before ending, about the Delta Kappa Epsilon performance the other night, which was very successful indeed, the Hasty Pudding Club last evening, also uncommonly satisfactory, and a little more devious than usual about College Matters, and how I am *trying* to think it is all "splendid" about Perry, and how he is still working and happy and interested, and first-rate, often talking of you and longing for you (though I believe he has been almost as naughty

as I, and has not written for some time), about the Everett Athenaeum, a revival of an old-fashioned (really) literary society, and how Perry and I went the other night to their public meeting—so charmingly, genuinely, earnestly Sophomorical, and yet with a certain higher note in it of manlier power—

Family relations had been strained, but improved with Ben's visit home in late fall, for everyone was immediately concerned about the state of his health. Here, he seemed to improve, but his condition worsened on his return to the mines in January and he died in Michigan the following April. We were all very sad. I tried to recall our pleasant times together in Europe, especially in Dresden, but I also remembered my visit with him later in Marquette, when I was completely unable to establish the old rapport.

FIVE
MORE SEX IN EUROPE

THE SUMMER OF 1869 was the nadir of my relations with Tom. I think he had not realised the depths of my feelings for him. When he returned from "circumnavigating" New England with Stratton and saw how disappointed I really was, he quickly attempted to make it up to me. Soon we were in our old rhythm again, enjoying plays and concerts together, and occasionally moments of wonderful love-making. I felt instinctively that this situation could not last, yet I also felt sure of Tom's affection, that I would never lose it. Tom's feelings for me did not match mine for him, but he was very sensitive of my feelings and was now always careful not to hurt me. And although he was used to being admired and praised, I think he valued my opinion of him most of all.

That year also marked a turning point in my relation to Harvard, when Charles W. Eliot was elected president, replacing President Hill, who had resigned the year before.[1] Eliot immediately saw to it that I was made University Professor of Mathematics, thus assuring a permanent position for me. We were then thirty-one on the faculty, of which over half (18) of us held the rank of professor. He also

---

[1] Thomas Hill (1818–1891), Unitarian clergyman; president of Antioch College (1859–1862) and Harvard (1862–1868).

discussed with me his plans for developing Harvard University, especially graduate instruction, and asked my cooperation. I gave it readily; I shared his vision of the academic future of Harvard and I knew from experience that I could work well with Eliot. That project came to first fruition in 1872 with the establishment of the Graduate Department, whose executive officer I was for eighteen years; and when it officially became the Graduate School in 1890, Eliot named me its Dean, a position I held for the following five years. Thus, I think I can rightfully say that I was "almost the father" of the Graduate School. But I am getting ahead of my story.

Although Eliot did not promote Tom to instructor, as I had hoped, he did recognise his linguistic ability when, in February 1870, he invited him to give a course in Sanskrit. Tom told me of the invitation in a letter of mock excitement on February 14. I recall the date exactly, for the letter began, "My dear Valentine." The opening had special meaning for me, of course; Tom well knew how much I liked it when he was "sweet." (Alas, when the course was finally offered in the summer of 1871 only one student showed up for the class. Tom persuaded him to give up Sanskrit.)

In the summer of 1870 I returned to Europe, going to London for the first time. My brother Charles crossed over with me, but we separated upon leaving London. Or rather, when he left London, for he was anxious to get to the Continent. I was not sad to see him go. I recognise his brilliance, and he can be charming, but as a traveling companion he is very irritating, never sticking to plans, always acting on whims regardless of the desires of others. Besides, he did not share my love of the theatre and I wanted to take in what London had to offer, which was much indeed. It was on my arrival in London that I first experienced the pains that were later diagnosed as gallstones.

At the time, however, the pains did not last and I attributed them to indigestion.

It was also during this stay in London that I first heard the name of Karl Heinrich Ulrichs. During the intermission of a concert I had entered into a conversation with a young man of almost feminine beauty, whom I found strangely attractive. He invited me to join him afterwards at a small party at the house of a friend, whom he only referred to as "Viola." I did not know what to expect there, but somehow I was not surprised to discover that Viola was not a woman, as the name would indicate, but a man. My companion, too, who had introduced himself to me as "Henry Maltravers," was also known in that circle as "Kate Smith." It was my first contact with a group of effeminate homosexuals. Maltravers had sensed the sexual element in my interest for him and had supposed that I was like him. I had, of course, wondered about my own makeup, but had not really found anything distinctly feminine about myself—except, of course, the fact that I was attracted to men. I did not think of myself as a woman. Everyone else in this group, however, apparently did, and Viola immediately began to explain to me the theories of Ulrichs, which seemed to me a bit confused.

The confusion was due in part to Viola's explanation, for he was still recovering from the death only a few months earlier of a young man who had shot himself in despair. He had been hopelessly, as he thought, in love with Viola; but after the tragedy, Viola devotedly nursed him until his death. The explanation of his own make-up given me by Viola was, to be sure, essentially that of Ulrichs, but colored by his recent experience, and I could not see a clear plan in it. Still, it raised new questions about myself and I wished to learn more. Viola had his information second-hand, for he did not read German and his acquaintance, who, he said, had a copy of one of Ulrichs's booklets, was no longer in London.

The evening was interesting and I would have liked to have known the group better, but in fact they seemed more interested in discussing an upcoming ball to which they all planned to go dressed as women. I had not dressed as a woman since Hasty Pudding days and had never tried to really fool anyone into believing that I was one, but this seemed to be the point of their activity—what sexual outcome they expected was not at all clear to me. At any rate, I left London for Germany before the date of the ball determined to try to find out more about the theories of Ulrichs, to find some of his booklets, if possible, for I knew of no discussion of attraction between men since the time of the ancient Greeks that was in any way positive. I was eager to find a discussion that was not couched in religious terms as it always seemed to be in New England.

[The following is from Peirce's diary.]

The name Werner Eschholz zur Hohenburg had been brought to my attention as some one interested in discussing attraction between men, and since I had to spend several days in Freiburg anyway, I wrote ahead to Werner, giving him the address of my hotel and suggesting that he write me there and suggest how we might get in contact. I heard nothing from him and assumed that he was not interested. Then one morning at breakfast I was handed a note from Werner, who had come by the previous evening and urged me to contact him. I sent a message asking him to come to my room at the hotel at 3:00 p.m. the following Sunday, to which he agreed.

All Sunday morning I was excited, wanting not only to discuss the topic, but hoping that the young (as I had been told) man would be attractive and would be interested in me. Finally, punctually, there was a knock on the door. I answered and nearly gasped when I saw the handsome, sturdy man, who had a friendly voice and manly handshake.

Our conversation quickly disclosed, however, that the young man (who turned out to be thirty-eight, but looked several years younger—I took him for thirty) was a lover of boys and, as he emphasised, unable to feel sexual interest for an older man. Here was yet another species, entirely different from the group in London! Was there anything we all had in common?

Our conversation was pleasant, however, and I enjoyed being in the company of the charming Werner; I soon suggested that we use the familiar pronoun "du." It had rained since noon, so we had stayed in my room instead of going out, but the rain having stopped, Wer ner suggested that we go for a coffee. I said that I had eaten little lunch and suggested an early supper together. It was finally agreed that we would go first to Wer ner's house for coffee and then to a restaurant, which we did. I spent some time looking through Werner's library of novels touching male interest (some of which I already had in my own library) and we argued the relative merits of some of them.

Shortly after leaving the restaurant Werner once again mentioned his hobby, massage, and offered me a massage as a "farewell" gift. I gladly accepted, thinking, "If I can't have him in my arms, I'll at least have his hands on me, and if I have an erection, well, he will see that I told the truth when I said how attractive I found him." Thus, when we reached Werner's house, I quickly slipped from my clothes and awaited his instructions. He also stripped completely nude. I was surprised by this, but enjoyed looking at him.

On Werner's instructions, I lay on my stomach in the middle of his bed, while he splashed oil over my back and began the relaxing massage. He worked from one side and then the other. Next he straddled me and worked over my neck and upper back. I could feel his penis dangling between my own buttocks and, as my excitement grew, felt my own penis lengthening, even though it was pinned beneath me. I sighed my contentment.

By the time Werner told me to roll over onto my back, I was already semi-erect. Now I became more erect as he massaged around and over that region, seeming to touch my penis only in passing, almost accidentally. I indicated my pleasure at every touch. Soon it seemed that he was concentrating his attention there, with one hand on my penis (with just the lightest touch, however) and one hand, or finger, on a nipple, as if to distract me from the real center of interest. I had closed my eyes, but now opened them and watched his face. Indeed, he did seem to be enjoying what he was seeing. I again closed my eyes. By now I was firmly erect and felt an impending orgasm welling up in me. It was a pressure, almost painful, but exquisitely enjoyable. I wanted it to continue, and yet, every time Werner released his touch, I wanted only for him to return there —and he did, with the most delicate, tender caresses.

Finally, my body could contain itself no longer. "I'm coming," I said (or rather "Ich komme," since we were speaking German), as the first drops welled up and spurted out. Now Werner firmly grasped my penis and pumped out the rest of my ejaculation, then with a towel he quietly wiped it and his hands dry of the semen, and just as quietly said, "Now I'll lie down awhile." He stretched out on his back, next to me, keeping one hand on my thigh, fingers in my crotch. I rolled over on my side, said "Thank you," and laid my head on his chest, my arm grasping his shoulder. How beautiful life was, and how beautiful and generous Werner was! I was overcome by a great happiness. I raised myself on an elbow and tried to tell him of it, but I knew my words were inadequate, and I could only hope that he could realise how I felt. I lay down again, face down and next to Werner's face (wanting to kiss him and not daring to do so), while I grasped his shoulder tightly. I could have stayed there for hours, but I knew he had to get up early the next morning to go to work. So we dressed and he took me back to my hotel. We promised to write and, if possible, to meet again. There was a farewell hand clasp (again I restrained my impulse to kiss him) and I hoped against hope that he could feel the depth of my gratitude.

Werner had predicted that I would sleep well after that "relaxing" experience, but in fact I slept little. It seemed that I did not need the relaxation of sleep. But I was happy each time I awoke during the night, for my thoughts immediately returned to Werner and the incredible, unexpected, and wonderful experience!

From Freiburg I went to Munich, where I attended several concerts and plays and discreetly inquired about the writings of Ulrichs, which I was still eager to find, although I felt that the experience with Werner in Freiburg was worth much more. None of the booksellers had any of Ulrichs's booklets, although one of them recalled that three years earlier a man with that name had caused a stir at the Congress of German Jurists meeting that year in Munich by proposing that sexual acts between men be decriminalised in all of Germany. "And why not?" the bookseller said. "Bavaria has been without such a law since 1813 and I don't see that things are any different here than in Berlin. In fact, I think they have a lot more of those people in Berlin than we do here." Neither he nor I knew that the legal situation would soon change, for even then the war was brewing that would lead to the unification of Germany and the extension of the Prussian law to Bavaria.

In fact, war was declared by France in mid-July and so I gave up my plan to go from Munich to Paris. That change allowed me to seek yet another "adventure" with Werner Eschholz zur Hohenburg.

I had written to Werner and had received such a nice reply with an invitation to stay overnight at his house, that I immediately made plans to return to Freiburg. Werner met me at the train station, his face glowing with friendliness. We walked to his house, relaxed over coffee, and then went out to dinner. On returning home there was less than an hour before his bedtime—I knew that he arose very early before going to work. I was afraid that he would think I had returned only for another "massage," so I carefully explained what I wanted from him, thinking he would not object: "After I clean my teeth" I said, "just let me lie with you and hold you for a while, and then you can go to bed." He agreed.

When we lay down, I saw that there was only a half hour left. Enough, I thought, I *will* enjoy it. We stripped to our undershorts, he lay on his back, I lay beside him, my head on his chest. "Are you listening to my heart?" he asked. "Mmmmmm," I answered. But I lay quietly, occasionally clasping Werner tightly. How wonderful to be with this beautiful man!

Soon, however, Werner's hand stretched to take hold of my penis. "Not necessary," I said, "I just want to hold you." But he insisted. Then, unexpectedly, he placed my hand over his own genitals. I was surprised by the move, but caressed him and began to move his penis out. He responded by removing his undershorts altogether, and I saw that he was beginning to have an erection. I slid down on the bed, laid my face in his groin, and took his penis in my mouth. It continued to grow as I became more active. "I must make more of an effort to please him," I thought, and I directed my attention to this. As Wer ner's erection reached its height, I noticed that I had lost my own erection and vaguely wondered why this activity was not more exciting to me. But I continued and was pleased that Werner was apparently enjoying my action. But I cannot continue longer, I hope he comes soon, I thought. Finally, I could not continue, stopped and told him so. "Will you come?" I asked. "Yes," said Werner, "but you'll have to work longer." I did, but was again exhausted. Werner masturbated himself for a while, but then said it wasn't the same and asked me to masturbate him. I did, laying my head on his stomach. This way I could continue longer. All the same, I grew tired. But finally he began to have a spasm. I put my mouth over his penis and sucked it in during several more spasms. Werner raised himself, kissed the top of my head. "Thank you!" he said. And twice he said, "Thank you for being patient." I relaxed, reassured and happy with the outcome. "Are you content with me?" I asked. "Yes," he said, and I drew myself up beside him, kissed him on the lips, and lay my face in the crook of his neck. I glanced at the clock and thought, I could lie here forever, but I've only three more minutes. It was not the relaxing half hour I had expected, but I was glad that I had been able to bring Werner to ejaculation.

"Now I will satisfy you," he said, but I was determined. "No," I said, "I promised you that you could go on to bed and I want to keep my promise." He was hesitant, but I insisted, extracting a promise from him that he would say good-bye before leaving for work in the morning. (I was to leave before he returned from his work.)

Werner kept his promise, and when he came to say good-bye he was entirely nude. He sat on my bed and smiled. I sat up, clasped him tightly and buried my face in his chest. "What a wonderful, beautiful man! How I could love such a man!" and other such thoughts raced through my head. But I knew I must force myself to release him. I watched Werner dress with greedy eyes and when he was finished, I clasped and kissed him again—and again.

After Werner left, I relaxed in bed, recalling my experience. I was determined to see him again. As if to reassure myself, I took out the photograph he had given me at my request. I thought, "It is a good experience. I will not forget this man."

After returning to Cambridge I wrote several times to Eschholz zur Hohenburg, but never received a reply. It was my greatest disappointment since the summer Tom toured New England without me. But whereas Tom later made it up to me and continued to be a wonderful friend, Werner simply vanished from my life with no explanation. I tried again and again to think of an explanation of his failure to respond, and could not. I still have warm feelings for him and can only wish that he found happiness with the boys I know he loved. How I envied them! If I were such a boy, how I would try to be nice to him and please him—but for me it was too late.

The next couple of years were busy and pleasant. Eliot was determined to push the development of graduate instruction at Harvard and I was involved in every step. In fact, I gave one of the first University Lecture series. But I also attended a course on Celestial Mechanics given by Father, who announced that he would give the course if three students could be found who were qualified to take it. Actually, I was not very interested in doing so, but William E. Byerly talked me into it.[2] He was very keen on the subject, as was Mary Whitney, the astronomer;[3] apparently no one else was, so that William insisted that I be the third, and he charmed me into it. After Tom, I think William was my ideal man, and I would have done much for him. We became good friends and, despite the fifteen years difference in our ages, I was soon confiding in him. William would not have welcomed sexual advances, I think, and I did not make any. But he understood me far better than some who have shared my bed. He was able to appreciate my interest in young men, such as he was; not only for the benefit to him, but because he saw it as a general good. He never hesitated to give me his support when suspicious rumors circulated about me. Nor did he find me unmanly. In short, he was quite extraordinary, and I knew

---

[2] William Elwood Byerly (1849–1935) graduated from Harvard at the head of his class in 1871; in 1873 he received one of the first two Ph.D. degrees from Harvard. After three years as assistant professor of mathematics at Cornell University, he returned to Harvard in that rank. He was promoted to professor in 1881, becoming Perkins Professor of Mathematics in 1906 after the death of J. M. Peirce.

[3] Mary Watson Whitney (1847–1921) was professor of astronomy and director of the observatory at Vassar College (1888–1910). Dell Richards put Whitney in the list of "Spinsters Who Need to Be Researched" in her *Lesbian Lists: A Look at Lesbian Culture, History, and Personalities* (Boston: Alyson, 1990), p. 105.

how to appreciate him. We even got along mathematically (impossible with Tom!), for William was a superior student then and the best of colleagues now. I have let it be known that I wish him to succeed me as Perkins Professor on my retirement in 1907, when I shall have given fifty years of service to Harvard.

I did not see Tom as often as I wished, but that was because I was as involved with administration as he was with his vast reading and his writing (he was already contributing to the *Nation*, the *Atlantic Monthly*, and the *North American Review*), and both of us were busy with our teaching. After the expected promotion to instructor did not come for him—Tom blamed Eliot, of whom he had a low opinion in those days—he had resigned his tutorship, so that when he was offered in August 1872 the assistant editorship of the *N.A.R.*, he immediately accepted. Well, not immediately, for I have a letter in which he said he wished to discuss the matter with me, but I think his mind was already made up and he only wished to share his pleasure. It is too bad that the position did not last more than a year; that was the beginning of a long string of bad luck for poor Tom.

Perhaps the most exciting event of 1872 for most people was the fire that swept through the business part of Boston for two days in November and destroyed hundreds of buildings. But that section was rebuilt in two years with a vastly superior appearance and few now even remember what it looked like before. Tom and I spent most of two hours the first evening watching the glow over the Boston skyline.

That was also the year that Eliot established the Academic Council and made me its secretary. My principal function was to be executive officer of the Graduate Department. Our first task was to formulate new rules for the A.M., Ph.D., and S.D. degrees. The old A.M. "in course," which was my only "advanced" degree, was discontinued.

It had regularly been granted three years after graduation upon application and payment of five dollars. We awarded our first two Ph.D.'s the following year; I was delighted that one went to William Byerly.

The following years saw the process of liberalisation at Harvard continue under Eliot's leadership, and I am proud to say that I contributed to the progress achieved. It was I, for example, who proposed in February 1873 that required attendance at prayers be discontinued. I recalled that I had been reprimanded more than once for non-attendance when I was a student; I was convinced then that required attendance was merely counterproductive.

The whole year 1873 proved to be exciting for Tom. That was the year he became assistant editor of the *N.A.R.* and engaged to Lilla Cabot.[4] I greeted the first event with pleasure, since it seemed to me to well suit Tom's abilities and I was confident of his success. The second event, however, was very difficult for me to accept. Tom knew I would be happy *for* him, but he also knew that I would be unhappy at another decision of his. Namely, he thought that we should give up any further sexual intimacy. Somehow I had expected my intimacy with him to continue on and on; I suppose I had refused to let myself think about the possibility of its coming to an end. But a couple of weeks after my birthday in May he revealed his plans to me. He had not thought that he could ever love a woman, not enough to marry her at any rate, and was taken by the possibility of leading a "normal" life. Of course, I wanted his happiness, but I wanted to be a part of it—and now? I felt very abandoned, and I told him so, as I told him everything. I cried and so did Tom. Our tears were bitter, though his were tears of

---

[4] Lilla Cabot, painter, was the daughter of the Boston surgeon Dr. Samuel Cabot. She was three years younger than Perry.

joy. Despite all his assurances of unchanging friendship, I felt that my world had collapsed. I must have shown it far more than I thought, for he wrote a consoling note the following day. By then I had recovered somewhat and was able to return the sentiment in it.

> Cambridge, May 17, 1873
> Dear Tom,
>
> Of course I knew that tears of joy don't last long. But then they are as bitter as any when they are a shedding, and I was glad to hear that you had dried them and were enjoying the deliciousness of a clear spring sky. I am so glad you are so happy. It makes life seem less cruel to me, even if it has no mercy for me, that you have found its only joy.
>
> I had a charming call the other day. I was received so sincerely and feelingly and in a way that seemed to make me really a sharer in your joy. Our friendship is among the things I value most in life, and I like to think that now its pleasure is to be heightened for all coming time. I am apt to dread my friends' friends, for you know how few people there are who can like or understand me. But here I feel that I have already a strength which you have given me.
>
> Of course the above is not meant to be answered.
>
> Your affectionate J.

Henry James was in Switzerland at the time and heard of the engagement only indirectly. I dare say he too had mixed feelings about it, though he wrote a cheerful enough letter, which Tom showed me. Although subject to it himself, James' views on sexual attraction between men were, I believe, a good deal more conventional than mine.

I knew Miss Cabot only slightly at the time, but became much better acquainted with her by the time of their marriage in April 1874. I found her an excellent person in every way, and I was tremendously gratified by the matter-of-fact way that she accepted me as a friend. If career moves were unlucky for Tom, he was certainly lucky in his choice of a wife.

After several years of writing, which was of a high quality, but did not bring an adequate income, Tom accepted an offer of an Instructorship in English at Harvard in 1877, but that position, too, was not permanent. Tom was soon in difficulties over his method of teaching, and in 1881 Eliot refused to renew his position. That his teaching was effective, however, is shown by the fact that at the petition of the students he became a University Lecturer for another year, and the following year he taught a course at the newly established "Harvard Annex," or the Society for the Collegiate Instruction of Women, as it was officially known. W. E. Byerly, who became an assistant professor at Harvard in 1876, was one of the incorporators of the Society (in 1879) and the first Harvard professor to agree to give courses to women; he taught there ten years.

The year that Byerly returned to Harvard was also the year I began giving regular instruction in quaternions. Father had pioneered the study of that branch of mathematics in America in 1848 when he first offered a course including "Hamilton's researches respecting quaternions." He was again lecturing on quaternions at that time, but I gradually took over, so that from 1878 my course occupied two years. Interest in that subject has died down in recent years, being replaced by the popularity among physicists of Gibbs's new "vector analysis," but I still think the mathematical theory of quaternions far more elegant; and I should not be surprised if there were to be a resurgence of interest in the subject in the next few years.[5]

I was much concerned at that time to give a methodical, understandable introduction to the subject, for the major complaint against the theory was the advanced nature of Hamilton's treatise. My brother Charles wrote me in the winter of 1877 that he was glad to hear that I was making an Introduction to Quaternions. In fact, that project never came to fruition, but my article on "Quaternions" in *Johnson's New Universal Cyclopedia* that year has often been praised as the very best short introduction; indeed, I received a number of letters from readers expressing their gratitude. Many said that they had tried to read other explanations, but were only confused, that the subject became clear only on reading my little article, so that I think I may justly be proud of it.

In the summer of 1878 I again returned to Europe, spending much time in Paris, which I had been forced to pass up on my last visit. I was astonished at France's recovery from the calamitous war of 1870–1871; indeed, the Paris Exhibition of 1878 was an object lesson of the recovery. It was on a far larger scale than any previous exhibition and there were thirteen million paying visitors. The French exhibits occupied about half the space; all major nations, except Germany, were represented. I especially admired the Trocadero Palace on the northern bank of the Seine, which was erected for the occasion and afterward purchased by the city of Paris. Of course, the offerings in the concert halls and theatres of Paris were more abundant than usual; it was a great feast for me. The city itself seemed dirtier than I remembered from my first

---

[5] Contrary to Peirce's expectation, the theory of quaternions never returned to favor. See appendix C for a brief introduction.

visit, but—in the words of a French king —"Paris is worth a mess."[6] Most exciting, however, was an "adventure" on the train when I left Paris to relax for a while in the South. It was a chance encounter with a man who later attained a high administrative position in his home country, Senegal.

[The following is from Peirce's diary.]

I have to record a most unexpected and charming experience on the train south from Paris. I had taken a berth in an overnight sleeping car and when I prepared to retire for the night I met my compartment companion, a tall and strikingly handsome Negro, a Senegalese, as he told me. There was a slight hint of the Arabic in his face; in fact, his tribe was Muhammadan. He spoke French perfectly, much better than I, and after introducing ourselves we were soon in a brief, but engaging conversation. He was Georges Lupin— at least that was the French form of his name—and he had spent the past year in Paris training to be an administrator in French West Africa. His home was in St. Louis, which is situated on a island near the mouth of the Senegal river; it is the capital of the French colony of Senegal. After his schooling he was for several years a clerk in the municipal government of St. Louis, or N'dar, as it is known to the natives. There his honesty and efficiency were recognised,

---

[6] Peirce is making a pun on the phrase "Paris vaut bien une messe" (Paris is worth a Mass), which is attributed to Henri IV (1553–1610) at the time of his conversion to Catholicism in 1893. That action overcame the remaining opposition to his assuming the throne of France.

and he was sent to Paris for further training. He was now returning to Senegal to assume an administrative position. Essentially, if I understood him correctly, he is to be the liaison between the governor-general of French West Africa and various local govern ments.

Georges is obviously a very intelligent man who takes the duties of his office seriously; while in Paris, he also took advantage of the many cultural opportunities. In fact, we discovered that our paths had almost crossed already in several theatres. But he was anxious to return home; he thought a year away long enough. I went to bed thinking what a really nice man he was, someone I wish I could get to know more intimately. I had no idea that I was soon to do just that. For just as I was falling asleep, or perhaps was already asleep, I felt a light tapping on my shoulder.

"Monsieur Peirce, are you asleep?"

I raised myself on one elbow. The light from the corridor came only dimly through the curtained window and I could just make out the form beside me. "No, I'm awake," I said. "What is it?"

"You are a nice man and I am very lonely. I need human contact. May I just hold your hand a while?"

I was so astonished that it took me a while to appreciate the situation. But I'm happy to say I did not hesitate. "Yes, of course." And I reached out to take his hand. He was now sitting on the edge of my bed, leaning over me slightly. I, too, needed human contact. Desire welled up in me. Silently I placed my other hand behind his neck and gently pulled his face down to mine. He did not resist; obviously this was also desired by him. Our lips met, our mouths opened, our tongues caressed. By now he had dropped my hand, his full weight was on me, and he held me in a tight embrace.

"Take the covers off and crawl in with me," I said. Before he did so, I slipped out of my underwear and he did the same, so that we were soon naked beside one another. I ran my fingers over his arms and chest and thrilled to the touch of his smooth skin over well-defined muscles. "You are an athlete," I said.

"Yes," he said. "And you appreciate an athletic body." We both laughed at his impudence. How relaxed we already were with one another! And I did appreciate his body. My fingers trailed down his chest and stomach, the smooth expanse broken by patches of hair, not coarse and wiry, but soft like cotton. He relaxed onto his back as my hand continued further over his pubic hair and touched his penis, which gave a slight jump at my touch.

"Even that part is athletic," I laughed, and added, "I appreciate that too." I wrapped my fingers around his penis, which was beginning to stiffen, and rubbed my thumb over the tip. He was circumcised, as all Muhammadan tribes are, and the glans was completely uncovered. How smooth it was—and perfectly shaped. I felt my own penis stirring. Georges must have sensed it, for his hand soon covered my groin, which he caressed in several places at one. The effect was delightful.

I felt a wave of affection for this beautiful, lonely man. "Georges, mon petit Georges," I murmured. I think he understood fully, but he took it very lightly.

"Petit?" he asked. "And just where do you find me 'petit'?" We laughed. He was, after all, several inches taller than I am, his chest was twice as muscular as mine, and his penis was . . . proportional.

I squeezed and said, "Not there, at any rate." And when I slipped my hand down around his testicles, I found no smallness there either, for they were large and heavy, a beautifully matched symmetrical pair. It occurred to me at that moment that his whole body was completely symmetrical, with a symmetry that could be appreciated even math ematically. But I was no mathematician in that moment; I was a human being with a need for affection and, yes, with sexual desires. Any last bit of hesitation I may have had vanished, and I took from him—and gave—everything he and I wished.

It was a glorious night. It was well after midnight before we fell asleep in one another's arms. Our sleep was brief, but we awoke refreshed. Before dressing he rumpled his bed. That action was necessary, of course, but I almost regretted it, for I wished to proclaim to the world my pleasure in that wonderful man. But I knew that the world would not understand. We had shared our desires and needs, and had given one another pleasure and satisfaction. How could anyone find fault with that? Where was the harm? I knew too that I would not see him again; we both knew that. We knew it from the beginning and had accepted it. I'm sure we both thought, "Keep it light." Thus we were able to enjoy our breakfast together shortly before reaching Marseilles.

When we left the train, Georges took a cab directly to the harbor to board the ship that was to take him back to Senegal. As we said good-bye he took my hand in his, just as he had done the first time only a few hours before, and held it for a moment. "I shall not forget you, Jimmie," he said.

"I know," I said, "and I shall not forget you Georges," and I slyly added, "mon petit." On that light touch, we parted. He gave a last wave of his hand as his cab drove off. Oh, such experiences make life worth living!

I heard of Georges Lupin only once after that chance meeting on the train. Just last year there was a small item in the newspaper about a travel accident in Senegal and on the list of distinguished persons who died was his name. I was surprised to learn that he was survived by three wives and nine children. Was he already married, I wondered, when I met him? Did it matter?

SIX
HOMOSEXUAL THEORY

THERE WAS A good deal of talk about my keeping a room in Harvard Yard until I was forty-five years old, but apart from occasional writings in the toilet of the library little came directly to my attention. Some of the unpleasant remarks there may have been occasioned by poor marks in my mathematics classes, but some were unmistakable:

> Peirce is a sodomite
> Is JMP normal?
> Jimmie is a head-worker.
> The message is terse: Don't bed with Peirce.

It was there that I first saw the slang phrase "head-worker," but I knew immediately what it meant. How simplistically and hatefully it degraded what, after all, was a perfectly natural way of making love. I hated to see these comments and avoided going to that toilet. Still, the last one mentioned at least had the redeeming feature of showing the correct pronunciation of my name. (For this I preferred Tom's ditty: "Tell me student, which is worse: English with me, or math with Peirce?")

My friends were more concerned about the limitation of my living space, but in fact I managed to entertain by sending out for food. I recall in particular a lunch in May 1879, when my brother Charles was in Cambridge. Present, besides Charles, were Tom, John Fiske,[1] and J. K. Paine[2]—a most distinguished gathering! Fiske was still librarian at the time; soon afterwards he began his lecture tours which had such a tremendous success. Paine was already a professor for three years and had the distinction of being the first professor of music in an American university. I provided the food and cigars, and joined in the conversation. Charles was on his best behaviour; it was a memorable occasion indeed.

That was, however, my last large-scale entertaining in Holworthy Hall. The following year Father died and I moved from Harvard Yard to assume the responsibility of a house. Everyone thought it only natural that I should do so, since I was unmarried. I resented the assumption, but was in fact happy that I was in a position to look after Mother.[3] As it turned out, we got along famously, for she allowed me to handle all financial affairs without question. Father had left her well provided for, but some active management of her investments was necessary. I was pleased that I could provide the service, and I was not inexperienced. Despite what I considered a low income from the university, I nonetheless had managed to set aside a regular amount and had made some conservative investments that proved to be surprisingly profitable.

Nor did Mother ever interfere in my personal affairs. Of course I tried to be even more discreet than before, but I still had occasional

---

[1] John Fiske (1842–1901), philosopher and historian. After being assistant librarian at Harvard (1872–1879), he took to the lecture platform, with great success. He was also the author of numerous books.
[2] John Knowles Paine (1839–1906), organist, music teacher, and composer. He taught music at Harvard (1862-1906) and was professor from 1875.
[3] Sarah Hunt (Mills) Peirce was the daughter of Elijah Hunt Mills, U.S. senator from Massachusetts.

visitors who went directly to my room and were not introduced to her. She never inquired about them. I never knew how Mother felt about my homosexuality, if indeed she knew about it. I think she simply accepted me at face value—the face that she saw—and thought no further about the matter. She was, however, very conventional in many ways, and if she did not always share the opinions of society, she very much valued the opinion of society. She was not an amoral person, but was really rather moral; except that the first commandment of her morality was discretion. The thing that mattered most to her was that the family stay together, that is, that there be no perceived breaks between family members. It was for her sake that I continued to put up with Charles's inconsiderate behaviour. For his part, Charles seemed to share Mother's point of view, which always seemed rather incongruous to me, although it did allow him to continue to insist that I support him financially.

With the death of Father, I became the only Peirce in the Mathematics Department, but that did not last long, for in 1881 my distant cousin B. O. Peirce joined us as instructor.[4] This was definitely not a case of nepotism (as my own position had often been thought to be), for he is a highly gifted mathematician and physicist, who merited the position then and continues to be a valued colleague. That was also the year that W. E. Byerly was promoted to a full professorship. Thus I felt that even with the loss of Father we had a very strong Mathematics Department.

I encouraged the idea of sharing our strengths with the Massachusetts Institute of Technology and this year (1881) the teachers of mathematics and physics of Harvard and MIT formed

---

[4] Benjamin Osgood Peirce (1854–1914). A Harvard graduate (1876), B. O. Peirce received a Ph.D. from the University of Leipzig in 1879. He taught mathematics at Harvard from 1881 to 1914, with the rank of professor from 1888.

the M. P. Club, of which I was elected president, an office I continue to hold. I think the informal contacts have been as important—for both institutions—as the formal papers read at our meetings. As I wrote Charles the following year: "I really think that Mathematics is beginning to take a stronger hold in this old bog of slushy unreality." (One had to take this rather self-deprecating tone with Charles, or else he would think it offensive boasting.)

In the summer I returned to Europe for a delightful round of opera and theatre in London and Paris. In the latter city I found a shop with delightful underclothing, which I later mentioned to Tom. We recalled the underwear he had bought in the Eternal City years before, whose color we ever afterwards called "Roman red."

Although I was generally pleased with the academic performance of our Harvard students in mathematics, in another area, their public conduct, I had no reason to boast. Oscar Wilde's visit to Boston in January 1882 was the occasion of a dreadful display of incivility. Sixty of them, dressed in a caricature of Wilde's usually rather flamboyant stage costume, had places in the front rows of the lecture hall and during his speech "hooted and hollered" disgracefully. But Wilde was equal to the occasion and handled them very well. He had got wind of their plan and dressed in ordinary trousers and jacket, and he made a few remarks about their being caricatures of aestheticism. They rather childishly began to applaud every time that he drank from his glass of water, but that did not gain the approval of the majority of the audience, so that in the end the students were quite chagrined. The newspapers had been generally hard on Wilde, but the Boston *Evening Transcript* declared that evening a triumph for him.[5]

---

[5] The extensive 1882 lecture tour of Oscar Wilde (1854–1900) through the United States and Canada is well described by Richard Ellman in his *Oscar Wilde* (New York: Alfred A. Knopf, 1988).

I thought Wilde brilliant and my admiration for the man was great. I regret that I never met him personally. I suppose I could have, if I had made the effort, but he was rather monopolised by such people as O. W. Holmes[6] and Julia Ward Howe.[7] Wilde himself insisted on meeting Longfellow,[8] who died later that year and was already too feeble to go out; I believe Wilde called on him for breakfast.

Like many others, I examined Wilde's features carefully to try to find evidence that he was "so," but I found nothing revealing. It was a shock to me when he was convicted in 1895 of homosexual offenses and given that barbaric sentence. He left England for the Continent shortly after his release, but I hear he is a broken man. When will the world ever throw off its barbarism and stop treating perfectly natural actions, harmful to no one, as heinous offenses?

The year that began with the brilliance of Oscar Wilde closed with another kind of brilliance, for it was in the winter of 1882–1883 that electric arc lights first illuminated the streets of Boston. It was quite an experience after kerosene lamps and gas.

In the spring of 1883 my brother Charles was divorced from his first wife, the former Harriet Melusina Fay. Zina, as she was called, was well known in Cambridge as a pioneer advocate of the

---

[6] Oliver Wendell Holmes (1809–1894), professor of anatomy in the Harvard Medical School, was a classmate and friend of Benjamin Peirce. He is best known as a man of letters. In one of his novels, *A Mortal Antipathy* (1885), Holmes showed an awareness, if little understanding, of the prevalence of homosexuality: "Among many other thoughts which came up was one which involved the suffering of multitudes of youthful persons who die without telling their secret: how many young men have a fear of woman, as woman, and in consequence of which sex attraction is completely neutralized." In *The Psychiatric Novels of Oliver Wendell Holmes*, abridgment, introduction and annotations by Clarence P. Oberndorf (New York: Columbia University Press, 1943), p. 247. In the same novel Holmes may have had Peirce in mind when he has a rather masculine female character become "engaged to a clergyman with a mathematical turn" (p. 254).

[7] Julia Ward Howe (1819–1910) is best known as the composer of *The Battle Hymn of the Republic*. She was a leader in the women's suffrage movement and participated in the move to promote international peace, in which subjects she lectured widely.

[8] Henry Wadsworth Longfellow (1807–1882) was professor of modern languages at Bowdoin College (1829–1835) and Harvard (1835–1854), but devoted himself wholly to his writing from 1854. His translation of Dante's *Divina Commedia*, a masterpiece of literal translation, gave a great impulse to the study of Dante in America.

organisation of women among themselves. As early as 1868 she had written in the *Atlantic Monthly* about the cooperative housekeeping so as to relieve women of housework and encourage their financial independence. She was a very strong woman and I often wondered why she put up with Charles' whims. In the end it was apparently too much for her. But if Cambridge society was shocked by the divorce, it was even more shocked by Charles' remarriage that same year to the Frenchwoman Juliette Froissy. Mother never forgave him—at least never to the extent of inviting Juliette to our home. At the time of Mother's death four years later my own relations with Charles were strained for other reasons, so that it was not until ten years after their marriage that I found an occasion to hold a reception for the second Mrs. Charles Peirce. That was in 1893, on the occasion of the Lowell Lectures in Boston, and even then only three of the ladies who were invited came. They were Mrs. Edwin H. Hall, who was a relative of mine on my mother's side, Mrs. B. O. Peirce, and the second wife of the late Professor Louis Agassiz, a lady with whom I have had the most cordial collegial relations since she became president of Radcliffe College when the "Harvard Annex" received that name the following year.[9]

The year 1883 was also a momentous year for me, even if there were no outward signs of it, for this was the year that Tom began his correspondence with John Addington Sym onds.[10] My own correspondence with him began somewhat later, but from the beginning Tom shared with me the views of Symonds on homosexuality and we had long discussions of it. After the guilt of my "religious" period, I

---

[9] Elizabeth Cabot (Cary) Agassiz (1822–1907) was a founder of Radcliffe College (1879) and its president (1894–1902).
[10] John Addington Symonds (1840–1893), English poet, essayist, and literary historian. His *Renaissance in Italy* (7 vols., 1875–1886) is a classic authority on the subject.

had completely accepted my own sexuality and indeed had read a few, very unsatisfactory books that touched on the subject (including Dr. Kellogg's quite dreadful book *Plain Facts About Sexual Life* of 1877),[11] but I had never tried to analyse it. I had always seen my relationship with Tom as something quite special and had not tried to generalise from it. Since Tom's marriage to Lilla in 1874 we had never again been sexually intimate; in the beginning this was very frustrating for me, but I had accepted it by that time and my friendship with Tom was in some ways more intense than ever. I felt confident that it was an enduring relationship—as indeed it has been. Tom, for his part, seemed to appreciate all the more my continuing devotion and we were able to share much. Certainly there were few with whom he could share his own liberal views on homosexuality.

Although Tom initiated a correspondence with Symonds in July 1883, it was not until the following year that Symonds, with some subtle encouragement from Tom, gradually came around to the subject of homosexuality. Even then it was an indirect mention of his book *A Problem in Greek Ethics*.[12] And Tom had to beg to see it. Symonds wrote him on March 22, 1884 (I noted parts of the letter):

> The Essay on Greek Manners which I told you I had
> printed privately is an attempt to analyse the social
> conditions & philosophical conceptions out of which
> Plato's theory of love as set forth in the Phae drus &
> Symposium emerged, & to compare that idea with
> the medieval ideal of Chivalrous Love. You will

[11] J. H. Kellogg, *Plain Facts About Sexual Life* (Battle Creek, Mich., 1877). In this book Dr. Kellogg only hints at the dangers of homosexuality. He finds the "solitary vice" horrible enough, devoting over 100 pages to it!
[12] In 1883 Symonds privately printed ten copies of *A Problem in Greek Ethics* .

understand from this description the reasons why I do not wish to give this study publicity. Unfortunately the English public is almost totally devoid of scientific curiosity. They cannot understand (no: not even after all that Darwin & Spencer have done for demonstrating the necessity of studying humanity in evolution) —they cannot understand that a man may take a philosophical interest in a subject for which he has no moral sympathy, & may think that worth analysis from which he would shrink in practice. They go on putting the Greek classics in the hands of their sons & encouraging the most hopeful youth of both sexes to penetrate its uttermost recesses. But they exact total silence upon the most significant anomaly in the life of the most brilliant race which ever occupied our globe—the race which has inaugurated nearly all our intellectual methods.

This essay is considerable in size: about 100 closely printed pages; & is the most learned of my writings. But I suppose it will never be read by anybody, even though it has been printed.

Of course we already suspected that Symonds himself was homosexual, and I found the letter somewhat offensive—even more so today when I am certain about Symonds. But that was his way. It seemed almost a necessity for him to persuade you that he had no personal interest in the subject whatever before he would discuss it in any way, and even then in usually disparaging tones. On the other hand, he welcomed and encouraged any revelation from others. Tom, however, was always more easy-going and accepting than I, and simply continued to insist on seeing the work. This continued pressure was really required, for Symonds wrote Tom on July 30, 1884:

> Do you really wish for my essay on Greek Morals? You must remember that it is practically an enquiry into the origin, development, & social relations of that unmentionable custom which perplexes every student of Plato. It is really dangerous in England to allude to such a subject, though every boy who gets a classical education becomes familiar with it. I shudder to think what the result would be if I were to divulge my treatise to the public—wholly analytical & scientific as its tone is. If after this warning, you would like to read it, I will send it, trusting to your discretion.

So Tom finally received a copy of Symonds's *A Problem in Greek Ethics* after much effort. It was probably the only copy he sent to America and shows, I think, what a high opinion Symonds had already formed of Tom—in part from Henry James, who had described Tom to Symonds as "perhaps the most learned man in America"— as Symonds had reported in his first letter to Tom. Of course Tom immediately shared the book with me and we had some lively discussions of it. Tom was quite taken by the literary references and quotations in it; I was perhaps more interested in trying to understand the practice of "that unmentionable custom" today. For this I found the life of the Greeks hardly relevant. And yet, it was a great comfort for me to know that somewhere, sometime there were people who felt as I did and could openly express their feelings.

The year closed with an indirect contact with Symonds when his friend Edmund Gosse gave a series of lectures at the Lowell Institute.[13] I went with Tom to hear him; O. W. Holmes was at every lecture, I learned, and was high in his praise of Gosse. For my part, I found him pretentious and took an instant dislike to him. Thus I heard only one lecture and met him personally only once. That was at a noon breakfast with him (Gosse had felt poorly and stayed in bed until midday). Tom also attended a reception for Gosse and had good things to say about him, but I found him rather sinister.

About the same time I became acquainted with another, quite extraordinary person, who was as yet unknown to the public. I mean Miss Emma Eames.[14] She and a few others had been hired by Professor Paine to illustrate his lectures on the history of music. Paine was quite taken with her talent and suggested to me that I might wish to sit in on a lecture or two just to hear her. I agreed to do so out of courtesy to Paine—and left the lecture completely won over to his opinion of Miss Eames. I immediately congratulated him on his "find" and together we predicted great things for her. It was not hard to do, for it was obvious to the two of us that she had a quite extraordinary singing ability and at the same time the sort of commanding personality that could demand attention on the stage. Of course we were right, as the whole world knows by now, and I am happy to be able to record that I have had the great pleasure of hearing her many times and of witnessing her operatic success.

---

[13] Edmund William Gosse (1849–1928), poet and man of letters. His American contacts are documented in *Transatlantic Dialogue: Selected American Correspondence of Edmund Gosse*, edited, with an Introduction, by Paul F. Mattheisen and Michael Millgate (Austin & London: University of Texas Press, 1965).

[14] Emma Eames (1865–1952), American operatic soprano. She married Julian Story, a portrait painter, in 1891 (divorced in 1907) and the operatic baritone Emilio De Gogorza in 1911. Her operatic debut was as Juliette (Paris, 1889); she thereafter appeared in London and New York during operatic seasons. Her scheduled appearance in San Francisco in 1906 was cancelled by an earthquake.

After Father's death I had become the head of the Mathematics Department. In 1885 I was also given his professorship, becoming Perkins Professor of Astronomy and Mathematics. The added income that the title brought made my "housekeeping" easier, but at the same time had the effect of straining relations with my brother Charles, who felt that he should share in my good fortune. He was never able to see that his difficulties resulted from his own actions: if he did not get the book contract he asked for, he saw an enemy in the publisher; if his family did not wholeheartedly accept his choice of wife, he saw us too as enemies. As for this last, I did what I could to stay on good relations with Juliette, but my efforts never satisfied Charles. And to give an example of his attitude toward publishers, he once proposed writing single-handedly a 100-volume encyclopedia—and was furious when the publisher did not give him an immediate advance to do so! He has undoubtedly a brilliant mind, but has had to learn—though I think never accepted—the fact that the world does not always reward genius.

With our family Charles was, to say the least, ingenuous. He demanded that we lend him large sums of money and was outraged when we asked for assurances of repayment. He expected us to take at face value his expectation of great financial reward from his next project. He became even more irritated when the time for repayment came and, as he did not pay, we asked for payment. This situation became aggravated during Mother's last year and would have come to a definitive break, I think, if our concern for her had not prevented it. By the end of the summer of 1887 Charles could write: "I was deeply attached to you all, but you have all behaved ignobly & contemptibly, & I will pay up what I owe & be done with you." Of course he did not pay; and "of course" I made another effort to preserve relations, sending him a gift for his birthday in September, with which I included bonbons for Juliette.

Despite my efforts, Charles apparently had one of his rages and dashed off a very insulting telegram to me. Even though Mother was already ill, that would have meant my break with him, if he had not written a letter of apology shortly after. I immediately replied with a conciliatory letter. Whether it was sufficient for a permanent reconciliation, I do not know; but the situation changed entirely with the death of Mother a few weeks later. I think he realised that he would have to deal more directly with me, especially since I was the executor of her estate. He also had the good sense to realise that I really was better in business matters than he, so that he entrusted me with certain decisions in the buying and selling of stocks that he had inherited. This I made very effort to do for his benefit. Thus our relations, which had appeared to be held together by Mother, actually improved after her death.

I think it was during this time that I realised how strong I really am. I had always been able to count on the moral and emotional support of Tom, but he (with Lilla and their three daughters) had gone to Europe in June, where he was to remain until late 1889, and so I was unable to talk directly with him about my problems. I missed him greatly, but I also saw that I could "survive" without him. I was not without some contact, however, for Tom wrote to me occasionally about his travels and acquaintances, particularly in the beginning. He first went to London for two weeks, where he saw Symonds several times—and no doubt charmed him, as he did almost everyone, for when Symonds contacted me later, he did so on Tom's recommendation. Tom also saw his old boyhood chum Henry James. He had looked forward to this, but the meeting was not entirely satisfactory. Of course he had not expected their boyhood intimacy to return, but I think he was not prepared for James's attitude. Tom thought him a bit aloof; I suspect James was embarrassed by the living reminder of his youthful enthusiasms. At any rate, it was the rare case when Tom's charm did not have its usual effect.

Alone with Tom, Symonds was able to discuss his interest in homosexuality at greater length than in his letters. Tom told him of my interest and wish that the modern period also be investigated. It was then that Symonds informed him that he was doing just that, was indeed preparing an essay on "Modern Ethics" to parallel his earlier essay on "Greek Ethics." Given his fear of how the public might react to the earlier book, his reticence about the second was not surprising. In fact, when he completed it in 1891 he had only fifty copies printed—a very limited edition! Still, Symonds recognised that Tom, with his vast knowledge of books, could be helpful, as indeed he was. It was Tom, for example, who in early 1888 called Meier's old article on *Paederastie* to Symonds's attention.[15]

In the spring of that year Tom and Lilla visited Symonds in Venice, where Tom again impressed Symonds with his knowledge of the subject—though I suspect not with revelations of personal experience, for Symonds seemed genuinely astonished when I hinted of such to him later.

During the summer university vacation I had another attack of gallstones, though this was not certain at the time. My physician Dr. Nichols had some suspicion of it, however, and recommended a year of rest and change. But then the pain went away in time for me to resume my usual activity at the beginning of the fall semester. I have,

---

[15] M. H. E. Meier, "Päderastie," in *Allgemeine Encyclopädie der Wissenschaften und Künste*, 9 (1837): 149–188.

in fact, been troubled with various bouts of illness in my life, but oddly they were so timed that I seldom missed classes as a result.

I recall that fall as a glorious time for theatre, though I paid dearly for my indulgence. The great Coquelin was in Boston the first week in November on a grand tour of the States. I went to see him six times in one week—as I wrote Charles, "not exactly an easy pleasure for an old codger," for the result was a severe case of diarrhea. But I must have forgotten the pain, for when Coquelin returned for another week in March 1889, I went to see him another five times. I enjoyed him greatly, and fortunately this indulgence did not have the former result. Nevertheless I recalled Dr. Nichols's suggestion that a year of rest and change would do me good; he particularly urged me to take the waters at Karlsbad, which were said to be good for gallstones. I determined to take a sabbatical year away from Harvard and do just that. In the meantime, however, I was enjoying a unique affair that made me reluctant to leave.

SEVEN
THE ALSWORTH AFFAIR

THE MAJOR EVENT of 1888 for me was the advent of Graham Alsworth in the fall, though I did not realise at the time how significant the event was. In December, however, I began to write about him in a special diary.

[The following is from Peirce's "GA" diary.
The letters "GA" evidently stand for "Graham Alsworth."][1]

I met GA when he came to my office and asked to take a test late. He was dizzy from a medication his doctor had ordered. I was usually reluctant to accept such stories, but was so taken by his beauty and charm (and he was very respectful) that I agreed immediately. This also happened a second time. GA did poorly on both tests, and I thought he did not much care, since he never asked to have the tests returned.

During the final semester exam in December, my eyes kept coming back to GA, who was poring

---

[1] Given the intimate nature of Peirce's "GA" diary, there is no doubt that the name Graham Alsworth is a pseudonym. Besides, there was no student in the Harvard class of 1892 with that name.

over his exam. ("What a beauty!" I thought. "How I would love to hold him!" And I pictured myself in bed with that beautiful young man wrapped in my arms, knowing all the time it was impossible.

When GA handed in his exam and left, my eyes followed him out the door. I was surprised when he turned, just outside the door, and looked back at me with a questioning look. I supposed he had looked back by chance and was himself surprised that I was watching him. I smiled to reassure him, and he went on.

Only then did I look down at the papers in my hand, and notice a slip protruding from them. On it was written: "If there is anything I can do for extra credit this semester, please let me know." This was followed by a Post Office box number. The word "anything" was   underlined twice. I tucked the note into my pocket, checked to make sure that nothing else like this was with his papers, and tried to return my attention to the remaining students in the room. But when I went home afterwards I discovered I was trembling, and after dinner I was unable to read as usual. My thoughts were   entirely occupied with GA and the question whether something was really possible after all.

There were, I knew, those at the university who would be willing to use a student to entrap me. The possibility was remote, but had to be considered. I therefore made no effort to contact GA, and would not have tried to contact him in writing in any case. Nor did he contact me; but when I made up final grades for the semester, I raised a grade on one of the tests I had never returned to GA (I then destroyed the test) and scaled the grades up, with the result that he passed the course. I wanted to help an obviously desperate GA. "And besides," I thought, "maybe he will be grateful."

By the beginning of the spring semester, in early January 1889, I had calmed down, and did not expect GA to contact. me. Then, after one of the first classes, he was the last student in the classroom to leave. I saw him looking at me, so I smiled to reassure him. When he walked over to me, I said, to further reassure him, "I destroyed the note." To my surprise, his reply was to ask, "When can we get together?" Hardly the reaction, I thought of someone who received a barely passing grade, so I asked if he knew his grade already. He did and was satisfied with it, and he repeated, "When can we get together?"

My fear of entrapment came back to me. I told GA that nothing was required of him. "But I want to," he said. I would not let myself believe that he really meant he wanted anything more than help with his homework. With resignation I said, "I'll be happy if you study and do well on your tests." And I walked away from a somewhat bewildered looking GA. I spent another trembling evening. I thought, "I have now cut off any possibility of getting together with him—but was there really ever a possibility?" By then I also thought, perhaps rationalising my actions, that I did not wish to go to bed with someone who did not really want to, but was only doing it because of a bargain. At least I could ask him for a picture of himself, I decided. So the next day I planned to ask GA for an interview, and I had to do it in such a way that he would not think I was trying to entrap him. I carefully rehearsed what I would say, but GA did not attend that class. At the next session, I waited by the door. When I saw GA, I said, "I *would* like to speak with you. Can you come by my office sometime?" (I thought the accent on "would" softened the tone.) "Sure," he replied, and continued on.

It was several days later when GA appeared at my office. I carefully explained that nothing was required of him, but I confessed that I had been attracted to him from the time I first saw him. "Your note was as if you were reading my mind," I said, and then added, "but I don't ask that of you. If you want to do something nice for me, give me a photograph of yourself." To my surprise, he did not accept this, and instead insisted that he wanted to get together with me. I was a bit nervous at this unexpected turn, but (carpe diem) said "O.K." GA asked, "When?" I suggested, "Tonight?" "Sure," he said. "About eight o'clock?" "O.K." As he started to leave, I couldn't resist speaking to him once more. "Graham? Thanks for coming here." "No problem," the young man replied.

I accomplished nothing the rest of the day, I was so nervous. I had said eight o'clock, so that I would have had my dinner, but now I knew I would eat little. I could hardly believe that GA was interested in sexual relations with me, and yet it appeared so. I still suspected blackmail, and I determined to find an opportunity to ask if he had had sexual relations with men earlier. GA arrived on time, I welcomed him, and we sat on the couch. At first we discussed the weather, but I maneuvered the conversation so that I could ask, "How old are you?" "Eighteen." "How old were you when you had your first experience with another man?" "Sixteen." I was greatly relieved by his candor about homosexual acts, and shortly after suggested that we go to bed.

I felt more nervous than GA appeared to be, but I knew I would have to take the initiative. The sight of his beautiful body was all I needed. I lay next to and partly on him, buried my face in the hair on his chest, and caressed his arms and chest. Later I moved down, kissed and took his penis in my mouth. Soon he lifted me off, and I returned to my former position, this time kissing his shoulders, neck, and lips. GA opened his lips, and we kissed deeply. Again I went down, and again I was lifted off. A third time, and now I could feel his balls tightening. He said "I'm coming." I made a noise to show it was O.K., and then tasted his ejaculation. I was elated that this had happened. Slowly I moved up again and clasped him in my arms. He returned the embrace, and we held one another tightly.

When we relaxed, GA began to stroke my back. I had lost all anxiety by now, for I felt that he was there because he wanted to be, and enjoyed what we were doing. To confirm this I said, "I'm glad you're here." He replied, "I'm glad, too."

Before GA left he asked if he might return. Nothing could please me more, and I said so. He bundled up against the cold weather outside and left. He had been with me an hour and a half. I poured myself a drink and relaxed in my chair, to recall and savour that glorious experience. Never had I been in bed with a man of such physical attractiveness, whose beauty was just at that heart-piercing stage between adolescence and young manhood. Such an unexpected experience at my age seemed incredible—and yet it had happened.

Ten days later GA asked to visit again that same evening. I happily agreed, and the evening was as enjoyable as the first. I was much more relaxed and made jokes several times, which he seemed to appreciate, although every time he tried to laugh a cough came out. He was recovering from a cold he said. Again I was overwhelmed by his physical beauty, and completely charmed by his unexpected display of affection.

This time, after GA left, I even allowed myself to dream that the relationship might develop into a lasting friendship and that I might continue to see him occasionally even after he left Harvard College. I tried to picture him on the playing field, for he had told me he was a football and lacrosse player for the college teams. I had never seen a lacrosse match; I considered going to the next one. The football season had ended in December.

It is curious how popular football had become at Harvard. It was only fourteen years earlier, in 1875, that the first match between Harvard and Yale was played. I had heard much criticism of the roughness of some of the games; and although parts of the costume were padded, there was little protection for the head. I remember wondering if my young friend still wore a cap during play; many players had discarded their caps, depending on their hair, which they let grow long, for protection. Alsworth did not have the appearance of a "chrysanthemum head," as they used to be called, so perhaps he had kept his cap.

I also thought lacrosse dangerous (the image of a "crosse" striking Alsworth's beautiful face crossed my mind) and I once said so to him, but he assured me that the game, which I was not familiar with, was not as dangerous as it looked. Although lacrosse was old, its current popularity dated only from 1867, the year that Canada became a Dominion and the Canadian player G. W. Beers helped form the National Lacrosse Association of Canada.

[The diary continued three weeks after the previous entry.]

GA saw me walking across the Yard and asked if I would be in that evening. I said yes, and he said he would get in touch then. But he did not show, and I was disappointed. That was on a Friday. On Monday morning, however, he was in my office to apologise, saying that he had been called home on an emergency, and asked if he might visit that evening. I was of course delighted.

GA's visit that evening was brief, since he had to

attend a meeting of the lacrosse team later. This time I began to feel not only a great sexual attraction, but also a growing tenderness toward the young man. I wanted to kiss him, deeply. I did, and was moved by his return of the kiss as well as his caresses. Fully aroused, I moved so that he could hold my penis, and he gently massaged it. I relaxed and enjoyed the sensation of being held and manipulated by him. With a spasm I came very quickly. After a moment of utter relaxation, I used the towel I had placed beside the bed on GA's hand and myself. Then I stretched out beside, him, my face red with the blood that had rushed to it. What bliss to be there!

Soon, however, I wanted to share more with GA. I began stroking him and returned my mouth to his stiff member, where it had already been earlier. I felt it grow even larger and stiffer as one of his testicles contracted tightly to his body. His hips moved in apparently involuntary waves, his body tensed, and I tasted his sperm. I held him in my mouth quietly and felt his member relax. I moved my tongue slightly and realised he was very sensitive there now. I let it slide out, but kept my face buried in his body for a while, then laid myself half across him, with my face in that wonderful corner between his neck and shoulder. How firm his stomach muscles are, I thought. I said his name several times, tenderly. He responded by holding me close.

But GA had to leave, though he appeared reluctant

to go. I joked about his having to go out into the cruel cold. Clearly we both were happy over the evening, and I felt more and more comfortable with him. It was another evening to remember.

When I think back on that time, it occurs to me that Alsworth was circumcised. I recall wondering why, since he was not Jewish. In recent years the medical profession has been responsible for the considerable extension of circumcision among other than Jewish children. They recommend the operation not merely in cases of malformation, but generally for reasons of health, though I think they exaggerate the danger. Perhaps Alsworth was an early example of this trend.

[The diary continues.]

I did not see GA again for three weeks, and then when he asked to visit, I had a cold and had to say "no." I suggested that he contact me the next week. He did, on the last day before the Easter recess. I discovered, to my surprise, that I was again anxious and my face was hot with blood in the hour before his arrival.

When he arrived, however, I was quickly reassured, for directly he was inside the door and had removed his jacket, he embraced me very affectionately. He even rubbed his body very seductively against me. I could feel his beginning erection between us. "You get the horn the moment you walk in the door!" I laughed.

"Is that where the expression 'to feel horny' comes from ?" he asked.

"Yes," I replied. It struck me that this was the first time I had heard him even mention a vulgar expression.

After glancing through a couple of magazines on a table, he announced that he had to leave within the hour. We soon moved to the bedroom, where he quick ly undressed and stretched out on his back on the bed, a beautiful figure. I looked at him a moment, my breath caught in admiration—and anticipation. Then I slipped from my clothes and slow ly moved from the foot of the bed up alongside GA, who clasped me in his arms in a warm loving embrace. I made an involuntary sound and held him tightly. We lay that way a few moments, until a motion in his hips called for my attention.

As I moved down his body, he relaxed, but his penis leaped in anticipation. I took it in my mouth and cupped my hands under his balls. But he would not let me stay there. Apparently not wanting to climax so soon, he pulled me up beside him and over him again.

I told him of my growing tender feeling for him, that what had begun as lust had quickly evolved. I did not know how he would react, but he accepted this gratefully, as indeed he seemed to accept what I was most anxious about, the difference in our ages. Once more I could hardly believe my good fortune. I tried to store up the moment, knowing the impossibility of it. I told GA that I wanted to be able to recall the memory of this moment during my sabbatical year in Europe. He listened with interest to my plans, but found a year a bit too long to be away, to which I agreed.

But present time was growing short. I did not want him to leave unsatisfied, and besides, it was my pleasure to give pleasure to him. I moved once again to that center of sexual delight, which had become somewhat limp during our conversation. It soon picked up. I took all in my mouth. I would like to have lain for a while just in that position, but I knew that more was needed, and indeed, his hips began a slight seesaw motion. I flicked my tongue around the most sensitive part, and used other motions I knew would excite GA, who was soon moaning as his cock swelled larger. When it could not become any larger, it became harder. With a groan, he climaxed and I felt the spurt, tasted it, gagged slightly, but recovered quickly, and kept still so as not to pain the now hypersensitive member.

When he relaxed, I moved up and laid my head on his chest. He wrapped his arms around my shoulders, and we lay quietly until it was time for him to leave. To my delight, just before he left he announced that he wanted to return after the Easter recess. "Do you mean it?" I asked. He saw what it meant to me and held me again in his arms. "Yes, I'll be back." After he left, I returned to my bed, remembering his smell and warmth, and brought myself to a climax. I poured myself a drink, returned to my armchair, and savoured the evening's experience.

I scarcely had time to think of Alsworth during that Easter recess, for I was occupied for many days with a large evening reception for graduate students. It was the largest ever; over eighty people attended, and it was generally thought to be a very successful affair. But I never afterwards took on the responsibility of such a large reception. Coquelin had also returned for several performances the week before, but because of the planning of the reception I was unable to see him as often as I wished. Still, I did manage to enjoy several performances of that quite extraordinary actor. Even after classes resumed I did not see Alsworth again immediately. When I did, I was struck by the change in his appearance. In that short period he seemed to have passed over that peak at the end of adolescence which is often so poignantly beautiful, perhaps because it is so impermanent. He was still a beauty, but not the breath-taking beauty I first thought him. He was again satisfying, but was never again to be the incredible ideal I had pictured.

[The diary continues.]

Five weeks later GA asked to visit again. We sat side by side on the couch, my arm around him, while he read a magazine that was lying on the coffee table. Then he lay back and relaxed into my arm, but shortly after suggested that we go to bed.

In the bedroom I lit a candle while he undressed, except for drawers, and lay on his back on the bed, his hands behind his head. How inviting he looked. I could have enjoyed just looking at him, but I quickly undressed and slid alongside and half over him. As I did so he brought his arms down and wrapped them

HUBERT KENNEDY

around me in a close embrace. Both he and I were aroused; he helped me move completely on top of him and we pressed our genitals together. I kissed him on the lips. At this, he opened his mouth and, as I pressed in, his tongue was in my mouth—farther than I thought possible. "How passionate he is!" I thought.

I withdrew my mouth and, reversing my position on the bed, approached his cock, while exposing my own erect cock to his view. As I enclosed his cock with my mouth, he reached out his hand and began masturbating me. I hardly had time to release his cock and say "I'm going to come very quickly," before I did. He wiped himself off, and I returned to his arms and relaxed for a while.

But he was still erect and I soon returned to unfinished business. He moaned several times and finally came in a climax that choked me, and I gagged several times. I recovered quickly, but had tears in my eyes, so that he asked, "Are you all right?" I assured him I was, adding, "But you almost drowned me!" He laughed with me. Again we lay closely wrapped in one another's arms and kissed again. I thought this would be the last visit from him, since the college semester would soon be over, but when he left he said he was staying at the college a few extra days and would visit again.

Three days later he was back for his last visit. Our love-making was passionate and affectionate. We seemed to be very comfortable with one another. We kissed, long and deeply, and I took his cock even deeper into my throat. Lying in the reverse position beside him, his hand around my waist, I breathed his cock in and buried my nose into his crotch. As I felt his cock reach the constriction of my throat, I heard him moan in pleasure. I repeated my action until he was coming, and held his cock in my mouth until he lifted me from its tender head. I reversed position and lay stretched along and over him, burying my face in the curve of his neck and shoulder. He held me, hugged me, and caressed me. I tried to store up the memory. Was I in love with him? Possibly. But all I knew was that I was then and there happy. Doubts might come later, but at the moment he was all I had hoped for and I treasured the moment.

This time he stayed longer than usual and seemed reluctant to leave. We held one another tightly several times, interrupting our dressing. Even after he had opened the door to leave the house, he returned for one more quick embrace. I felt a tremendous tenderness for him.

After he left, I poured myself a drink, sat in my chair, and savoured the experience. Even the following morning waves of satisfaction went through me. I was very happy in our relationship. Shortly after he arrived, I had asked for his address. I meant to write to him during the year that I would be away. Would the friendship last? I wondered if he would still be at the college when I returned and, if so, would we still be close? It seemed to me too good to be true.

EIGHT
EUROPEAN SABBATICAL

ALTHOUGH I KNEW I would miss my evenings with Alsworth, I was very much looking forward to my sabbatical year in Europe. And I had high hopes for my growing friendship with Harry Clifford, who was to spend the summer with me. After graduating from MIT, Harry had been a graduate student at Harvard for three years as well as an instructor at MIT. I had great respect for his abilities and found him personally charming; thus I had suggested that he accompany me. He turned out to be a delightful traveling companion, and although our friendship did not have the sexual excitement of my affair with Alsworth, it had an intimate depth that I much appreciated. And it lasted, for this was not the last time he would accompany me across the Atlantic.

We sailed from New York near the end of June 1889, dining on the eve of our departure at Delmonico's in that city with my brother Charles and his wife Juliette.[1] I learned then that she, too, was planning a trip to Europe with friends. Little did I suspect that I would meet her later in Egypt! The dinner was a great success. The presence of Harry

---

[1] Delmonico's, the grand restaurant at the corner of Fifth Avenue and 26th Street.

put us all on our best behaviour, not least because of his very real charm. Charles subtly hinted that I was "showing off" my friend, but even he was disarmed by Harry; for her part, Juliette was captivated by him.

Our summer included a meeting with Tom in Paris, where he joined us for a couple of evenings of theatre and opera. How comfortable and secure I felt in the company of those two charming, younger men! For Harry, the "bright young physicist from MIT" (as I had described him to Charles), the highlight of the summer was our visit to the quaint university town of Göttingen in Germany, for there we were able to meet the aging Wilhelm Weber, who despite his eighty-four years seemed to take delight in encouraging young physicists.[2] Like most old men, he enjoyed telling stories of his youth; but unlike most, he had really exciting stories to tell. Harry's knowledge of German was excellent and he listened in rapt attention as Weber described the days of the "Göttingen Seven," when he and six other professors were expelled from their chairs for protesting the action of the king of Hannover in suspending the constitution. That had happened a half century earlier, in 1837, when the personal union of the kingdoms of Hannover and Great Britain was broken by the death of William IV; Victoria became queen of Great Britain and her uncle Ernst August, duke of Cumberland, became king of Hannover. Weber was the sole surviving member of the group of seven, which had also included the brothers Grimm,[3] best known in America for their collection of fairy tales, but known in Germany as philologists. After twelve years, the last half of which he was professor in Leipzig, Weber returned to Göttingen after the constitution was restored, following the events of the stormy year of 1848.

---

[2] Wilhelm Eduard Weber (1804–1891), German physicist. With Karl Friedrich Gauss (1777–1855) he investigated terrestrial magnetism and devised an electromagnetic telegraph (1833).
[3] Jakob Ludwig Karl Grimm (1785–1863) and Wilhelm Karl Grimm (1786–1859).

From Göttingen we went to Bayreuth for the Wagner Festival. I enjoyed it immensely, and would have enjoyed it even more if Harry had also liked the operas. Alas, Harry did not share my musical taste. What can I say? Some people simply do not like Wagner. Harry then left to return to Boston, while I joined Tom and Lilla (the daughters stayed in Giverny) for a trip to Holland. That, too, was a great pleasure, and I think Lilla and I came to appreciate one another much better.

When the two of them returned to Giverny, I went back to Paris for more theatre and, in October, had the pleasure of hearing Miss Eames again, this time as Marguerite in Gounod's *Faust*. She had come far since I heard her in Professor Paine's class on the history of music, though I admit to being somewhat disappointed. Her vocalisation as a singer was not as good as it should have been, and I did not think her power as an actress had much depth. But I should say here that my view changed considerably two years later, when I again heard her in the same role in London. Already, however, I remarked a peculiarity of her singing that I much admire. Whereas most singers pause before a trill, Miss Eames just flows effortlessly into them.

From Paris I traveled south and then along the coast into Italy and down to Rome and Naples. In December I was in Florence, where I had a severe attack of gallstones at Christmas. Fortunately an American physician, a Dr. Baldwin, was staying in my hotel, so that I did not need to consult an Italian. He confirmed Dr. Nichols's suspicion of gallstones and strongly recommended, just as Dr. Nichols had done, that I go to Karlsbad, which I did the following summer. After that, I never had an attack, only some threatenings, which were relieved by further visits to Karlsbad. There really is something in the water there.

It was mid-January 1890 before I felt well enough to be up and about. In my concern about myself, I had paid no attention to the local gossip and did not know that Peter Tchaikov sky, the composer, had arrived in Florence. I discovered him for myself one day as I was walking across the Ponte Vecchio. A small crowd had gathered around a rather striking gentleman at one of the stalls. As I passed I saw that he was admiring a ring, which he gently returned to its case. He moved on immediately and the crowd moved with him, so I went to the stall to ask who the gentleman was. The shopkeeper told me and pointed out the ring that the Russian had just been looking at. It was a signet ring, showing a young man in Roman dress, holding a pair of scales and standing on a snake. I found it very attractive and inquired the price. It was far more than I wished to pay, but I decided to indulge myself, to have the ring as a souvenir of my chance encounter and as a symbol of our shared interest—if I could judge by the appearance of the young men who seemed to be his favorites in the fifty-year-old composer's group of admirers. Tchaikov sky was still in Florence when I left; I later learned that he had worked on his opera *Pique Dame* while there.

By mid-March I was in Egypt, where I stayed a month and a half. I was most impressed by the sheer antiquity of the monuments. Somehow that atmosphere of serenity that seemed to surround them flowed into me. In a flight of poetic fancy, I even wrote Charles that "the glorious Egyptian heavens transfuse the very soul with Oriental calm. But no calm that living man can experience approaches the sublime sweet godlike serenity of the sphinx under the full Moon." On the other hand, I may have only felt serene after dismounting from the camel that carried me to the Sphinx, for the ride almost made me seasick. During the latter part of my stay in Cairo I saw Juliette several times, but hardly had time to speak with her, as she was with a group of friends who seemed intent on seeing as much as possible in a short time.

From Egypt I went to Greece and, meeting friends just starting for Constantinople, joined them for a brief trip there. Nearly a year later I was still under the spell of my travels, when I told the Harvard Club of New York about my year away from the university:

> It was my delightful privilege to drink anew at solemn Roman fountains; to stand, for the first time in my life, on the glorious Acropolis, gazing on the ardent blueness of the Saronic wave; to eat the lotus, resting on the warm and lovely bosom of the Nile, and filling myself with something of Egypt's ancient and immortal life and light.

I spent several weeks that summer in Karlsbad and believe the fame of the waters is well deserved. It is alkaline-saline, with traces of other minerals, and colorless and odorless, with a slightly acidulated taste, which is not at all unpleasant. I purchased a charming porcelain drinking cup (Trinkbecher) with a picture of the discovery of the Sprudel spring by the emperor Charles IV on it and brought it back to Cambridge with me as a souvenir, but for practical use I preferred the cups with handles, since the water really is quite hot. When it comes from the Sprudel it is 164 degrees Fahrenheit; the other springs are somewhat cooler. I had expected the stay to be boring, but in fact the management of the hotel where I stayed provided many entertainments in great variety. It had not been affected by the inundation earlier in the year, which had caused a great deal of damage in the region. Most important, however, my friend Auric Ostfries was there. I had met him during my first year in Europe in 1867. He was a graduate student at that time in Göttingen, where I had gone to try to improve my speaking ability in German. We had quickly become friends, though not as intimate as I had hoped. That was the time when I was trying to be more open about my sexual interests, and indeed I found him sympathetic; but while he too was attracted to males, I was much too old for him, for he was attracted to boys in the ages of 14 to 17. I met several of his boy friends, but did not find them attractive. At any rate, my lack of ability in German was such that I had difficulty talking with them. In fact, I had difficulty at first with Auric, for he spoke quickly while hardly opening his mouth. After a while, however, I grew used to his characteristic speech and was able to follow him, which was made easier by his patience with me. I have seen him on every trip I made to Europe and we have remained good friends. I was sorry that he, too, was having physical difficulties, but very glad to have him as a companion at Karlsbad; it made my stay all the more enjoyable. A couple of years later those weeks were still so vivid in my memory that I wrote up a brief account of them.

Karlsbad 1890

By chance a small group formed, which lunched together almost every day. It was a heterogeneous group and I sometimes wondered what it was that held us together. I had earlier eaten alone and at first welcomed the change. I soon became bored by it, but, alas, it was impossible to return to my former solitude without changing my mealtime to an inconvenient hour.

We were six: I welcomed, of course, my old friend Auric Ostfries, whose tales of his adventures with boys were a constant source of amazement. But since these could not be continued at table, we often were quite   silent with one another. Then there were two other Americans, both about my age. One, a chemist from New Hampshire, was delightful. He never let the conversation lag, which it often did when he was absent. His name, John Smith, seemed much too simple, but was a good New England name, of course. The other American was a wandering scholar, slightly older, who had written a biography of a well-known German physicist. I immediately felt that I had more in common with John Greymore, as he was called, and indeed I had no difficulty conversing with this self-styled philosopher-historian, though I quickly learned to avoid certain topics. Once I mentioned homosexuality; a look of terror came over his face and he quickly, and almost incoherently, began talking about another subject. I could only guess at the source of terror for this aging bachelor, who seemed to have no intention of returning to the U.S. And after stating our political positions, we discovered we were so far apart as to preclude any comfortable discussion.

I was most attracted to Smith, however, who resembled Tom in many ways. He was tall, slim with very attractive hips from which one's eye ranged to other parts of his well-proportioned body. He seemed to glow with health, and I believe he did lead an active outdoor life. He was, in fact, not here for himself, but for his wife, who took her specially prepared lunches in their room. He naturally spent much of his time with her. Otherwise I should have tried to become intimate, for I found him charming and myself in the best of moods when I was with him. He had probably not thought much about homosexuality, but seemed to have an instinctive tolerance.

The remaining two were apparently old friends and always arrived at our table together. Frau Graulinden was in her early forties and unmarried— my friend Auric was convinced that she had "set her cap" for him. She had intellectual pretensions, having written a book on Spanish geography, but one soon learned to take her learned pronouncements with a grain of salt, for she had the unfortunate habit of having an answer for everything and volunteered the most amazing bits of information. She was often wrong, but never admitted it and took any attempt at correction as a personal insult. She once sat through an entire meal with tears streaming down her face. Indeed, her moods spoiled the civilised atmosphere of several lunches.

Her companion was a pleasant if somewhat colorless man, who was of interest, however, because of his ancestry. He was Ernst August, the only son of Georg V of Hannover (who had been deposed by the Prussian annexation of Hannover in 1866), and was always referred to by the title Royal Highness.

In his forties, Ernst August had gotten the idea of taking a degree in history and this seemed to be the basis of his friendship with Frau Graulinden, who had assisted in the preparation of his dissertation. She also appeared to have otherwise taken him under her wing, for the Royal Highness was somewhat awkward in every day social contact. This was probably due partially to the polite treatment he was always given, but more likely mostly due to a very real physical awkwardness that resulted from his partial blindness. He had a very restricted field of vision and was forever bumping into things and people. His blindness was progressively getting worse and there was talk of a possible operation, but this had been indefinitely postponed until after the granting of his degree. His blindness had no connection, it seems, with the total blindness of his father, except that, as Frau Graulinden confided to me, "he was after all related to Queen Victoria." Her tone implied that this fact was sufficient to explain this and many other possible evils.

Physically, Ernst August was not unattractive. He was slim and sinewy, with a bright voice and a firm, masculine handshake. His hips were somewhat too wide for this flat buttocks, but he was always neatly dressed with a foulard scarf around his neck, and altogether made a quite pleasant appearance.

He could not compete in this department, however, with John Smith, whose broad shoulders were beautifully proportioned to his back, which curved sinuously down to his narrow hips and well-formed buttocks. His abdomen did not have the flatness that has become the fashion in recent years among your modern-day athletes, but rather had the healthy—and natural—rounded quality that one finds in the classic drawings of Michelangelo and is so noticeable in his famous statue of David in Florence. I found him irresistibly attractive and imagined myself in his arms, or he in mine. Despite the impossibility of realising this situation, I allowed myself the pleasure of indulging the feeling that seemed to   radiate from him to me. I dare say his presence did as much to lift my spirits as the waters did for my physical ailments.

When I saw him alone, we naturally spoke English. At table, however, the conversation was normally conducted in German. Although not as well read in that language as I, Smith was much better at making conversation and evidently enjoyed doing so. Ernst August was an especially good listener, although his "Ja?" as an exclamation of interest could be quite startling, since   it was a bit too loud and, because of his blindness, he turned and stared at one straight in the face as he said it. His own contribution to the conversation was to immediately ask if the food was to one's taste. He seemed to find it amusing that I always professed to have enjoyed it immensely—this despite the fact that we always joked about the "paper napkin noodles."

Once, however, Ernst August volunteered a story about "a certain Ulrichs" who, after the annexation of Hannover by Prussia had agitated for the return of Georg V. He was amused by the fact that when the police arrested Ulrichs and searched his house for incriminating documents they were surprised to find literature and correspondence dealing with the subject of homosexuality. My ears pricked up at this, but as the Royal Highness did not seem inclined to continue the topic, I did not pursue the matter. It was early the following year, when Tom lent me Symonds's *A Problem in Modern Ethics*, that I finally learned how important Ulrichs was in the discussion of this topic. I wished that I had asked Ernst August for more details, though I dare say his interest went no further than what he had related.

That the Royal Highness made a good appearance was not just my opinion was shown by a remark of Smith one day. The Germans had left the table early and I asked him, in English, "How do we call the scarf Ernst August wears round his neck?"

"Dashing!" he replied.

Smith himself was always neatly dressed and usually wore a cravat, while Greymore and I allowed ourselves an "American" informality. I most enjoyed seeing Smith in a sky-blue sweater that seemed just the right color for his rosy complexion and set off the blue of his eyes, which sparkled behind his glasses.

Although calling himself a philosopher-historian, Greymore seemed little interested in the family of our Royal Highness and indeed had some confused ideas on his country's history. This was revealed the same day that I asked about Ernst August's scarf. Smith had asked a question about the Thirty Years War and I deferred to Greymore, who gave an entertaining and probably accurate account. He then proceeded to add a story of how the kingdoms of Hannover and Great Britain came to be separated that had nothing do with that very simple event. I found Smith later to explain this to him, and as it also helps explain Ernst August's position, I'll relate the story here briefly.

After being united for over a century in the person of their king, Hannover and Great Britain were abruptly separated on the death of William IV in 1837. Under the British law of succession, the next in line to the throne was his niece Victoria and she became Queen of Great Britain and Ireland. The Hannoverian law, however, did not allow the succession of a female. There the next in line to the throne was Victoria's uncle Ernst August, the younger brother of her father, and he became King of Hannover. Thus the two kingdoms, which had been joined since 1714, when Georg Ludwig, Elector of Hannover (Hannover became a kingdom only in 1815), became George I of Great Britain, were effectively separated.

On the death of King Ernst August in 1851, his son became King Georg V and the latter's son—our Ernst August—became the Crown Prince. There, however, the effective succession ended, for Georg V was driven into exile on the annexation of Hannover by Prussia in 1866 and any return of independence to that Kingdom appears highly unlikely. But, while not pressing his claim, Ernst August has not entirely given it up. On the death of his father in 1878, he declared that he retained all rights, but was obviously hindered from enjoying them, so that for the duration of the "hindrances" he bore the designation "Duke of Cumberland, Duke of Braunschweig and Lüneburg" with the title "Royal Highness." This is the explanation of the somewhat anomalous situation of having a Royal Highness at our table who was neither king nor prince.

Ernst August did not discuss his family with us. It was thought, in fact, that he was enjoying a "holiday" from his numerous children—and perhaps also from his wife, although she was said to be entirely devoted to him. He had married Princess Thyra, daughter of King Christian IX of Denmark, in 1878, shortly after the death of Georg V, and they had six children. They had remained "at home" in the Villa Klusemann in the town of Gmunden, on Lake Traun, southwest of the city of Linz.

My friend Auric related to me privately an amusing story of Ernst August's mother, Queen Marie, that took place in an earlier, happier period when she and her blind husband were on holiday on one of the East Friesian islands. It seems that there was no place for the boat to dock and the Queen, who was quite fat, had to be carried to the shore. The sturdy native who had been chosen for the task noticed her fear of falling into the water and attempted to reassure her by saying: "Your Royal Highness is afraid. Your Royal Highness need not be afraid. I have Your Royal Highness' behind firmly in my grasp!" whereby he used a local—and very explicit—East Friesian expression for "behind."

Although quite thin, the Royal Highness had a good appetite and ate everything on his plate. He had an odd habit, after having eaten part of his food, of scraping the rest of his salad onto the plate with the meat and vegetables. I assume his was because of his poor eyesight and he could thus concentrate on it better. The skin of his face showed aging, but the back of his hands fascinated me: smooth skin and a supply of black hairs that were not bushy but each an individual. He wore two quite simple rings on his left ring finger, apparently made of white gold. One appeared to be a wedding band; I suppose the other was a Guelph heirloom. Perhaps it is described in the book he was having Professor W. A. Neumann prepare on his family treasures. Ernst August spoke of it with enthusiasm; he expected it to be published the following year.[4]

---

[4] Several such rings are described in W. A. Neuman, *Der Reliquienschatz des Hauses Braunschweig-Lüneburg*, mit 44 Holz schnitten von F. S. Bader (Vienna, 1891).

HUBERT KENNEDY

NINE
THE RETURN OF ALSWORTH

DURING MY SABBATICAL year in Europe I wrote to Alsworth twice, but he did not answer. I was very disappointed, but accepted the fact stoically. I supposed that he had transferred to another college. But he remained a beautiful memory for me. Thus, on returning to the university in the fall of 1890 I did not even try to learn if he was still a student. And I never saw him. About halfway through the fall semester, however, I inquired at the Registrar's office about him and learned, to my surprise, that he was indeed registered. I thought of trying to contact him but did not. Then three weeks later he called me on the telephone I had recently had installed in my house. He asked if he might come visit that evening. "Yes, yes!" I was delighted—and nervous. How would he look? Would he still be as attractive as he was earlier? Had I changed so that he would not want to be with me?

Five minutes after he arrived, however, I was reassured. He obviously wanted to repeat the previous sexual experiences, for although he eagerly asked for an account of my European trip, he was quickly satisfied by my brief outline of it. We retired to the 'boat' bed and it was as if only a few weeks had gone by since our last time together there. (The bed that I used on the visits from Alsworth had partly broken spring connectors, so that it rocked from side to side, leading to remarks about being on a boat, or falling off. Once he said to me? "One day we're gong to kill ourselves on this bed!")

[The "GA" diary continues.]

I lovingly and thoughtfully brought GA to a climax with my hands and especially my mouth. Then he quickly brought me to a climax, following which we lay locked in tight embrace. Afterwards, I several times   interrupted his dressing to embrace him, and each time he responded generously. I told him of my sentiment for him, trying not to become too serious. Keep it light-hearted, I thought. He seemed pleased, but gave little response. He did respond to my embrace when he prepared to leave and even initiated several embraces.

After he left I made myself a drink and stayed up late, thinking over the unexpected visit. Well, I thought, if proof were needed, that's certainly proof that his earlier visits were not made solely with the aim of improving his grade! I wondered when he would return. He said he would, and I believed him.

His return a couple of weeks later caught me by surprise, however, and was not the visit I had wished, for this time he did not announce himself and rang my doorbell after 1:00 a.m. I was sound asleep. At first I thought it must be a child's prank, and did not get out of bed. Then the bell rang again insistently. I got up, aware of my sleepiness and the cold. (The stove had gone out for the night.) I put on a robe and slowly walked to the door, the doorbell ringing again before I reached it.

I did not recognise him at first, as he simply stood there without saying a word. "Come on in," I said. He did so, and I lit a light. I was almost speechless with astonishment. At this hour of the night! I sat next to him and asked why he had come, but he only said, "I wanted to see you." My impulse was to ask him to leave and return another time. I tried to show him that this was an inappropriate time for a visit. But he, apparently wide wake, only sat there, refusing to speak. I thought, "You cocky bastard! You think all you have to do is sit there and I will give in to your charm." And then I did give in. I moved closer to him and he welcomed me with open arms.

I would have been content to remain in this embrace, but he pulled his shirt up, encouraging me to put my face there, and he guided my hand to a spot over his cock. I unbuttoned his fly and took it out. I kissed it and held it. He was apparently willing to stay there on the couch, but I found it uncomfortable, and having now decided to complete the sexual act, suggested we move to the bedroom and undress.

There, I wanted to embrace, but he soon insisted that I give all attention to his cock. I did so and thought that he would soon come, since he seemed so eager.

But no, I grew very tired and finally stopped my action. He briefly masturbated himself, but soon pushed me back into place and, for the first time, led my hand to his rectum. I tried to insert a finger, but could not. He was apparently satisfied with the effort, however, and with my renewed sucking and caressing of his cock, moaned and humped.

I was happy that he showed his sexual pleasure. (I contrasted this with my experience with Werner Eschholz zur Hohenburg, who would lie inertly, revealing no feeling until the moment of ejaculation.) But I was exhausted. I now lay with my head over his stomach and masturbated him with my left hand.

He finally came. I watched it spurt out, some splashing onto my face. I waited until the spasms stopped and a bit longer, then, telling him to stay there, went into the bathroom to get something to wipe him off. He followed me and did it himself. Then I said, "Get back on the bed and just hold me for a while." "Sure," he replied and immediately lay down. I lay beside him. He took me in his arms, rolled over on top of me, and fell asleep. "One thing's for sure," I thought. "He feels comfortable with me."

I knew that *I* would not fall asleep. Nor did I want to. I was glad now that he was there and tried to store up the memory of how he felt in my arms. I thought of the many times I had lain alone in bed, longing to hold someone like this. But in those dreams we were not on top of the bed covers as now in a very cold room.

He awoke freezing, of course, and stood up to go. I suggested that he could stay the rest of the night, but he said he had to leave since he had to get up early; he was going to a football match. The Harvard football season was over, but he said the team was traveling out of town to see other teams play. I threw on my robe again, while he shivered from the cold as he dressed. After a last embrace before parting, I said, "Graham, I *do* like you—but not in the middle of the night!" He laughed. "OK," he said, "and I'll call ahead. I'll see you again soon." And he walked out the door. I looked at the clock; it was past 3:00 a.m.

GA did return two weeks later, with prior notification and at a reasonable hour. As usual, he had to look through all of my latest magazines. I snuggled up close while he was reading and enjoyed his warmth. When he finished reading, I asked, "Do you want to go to the bedroom?" "No, I just want to relax." And he lay back. I lay close beside him, and we embraced. He clearly had an erection, finally indicating that he wanted me to touch it. Together we undid his fly and drew it out.   After a while he suggested that we go to the bedroom.

Naked in bed, I ran my hands over his body and we embraced. Then I got a jar of lubricant I had prepared. "Perfectly safe," I said, "and you can even eat it." I put some on my fingers, positioned myself over him and spread it around the glans of his penis and began to massage him. His moans clearly showed that he found this very pleasurable. I varied my action, trying to find the most sensitive spots, but yet trying not to bring him to a climax too quickly. I could tell that he was getting close when I felt his right testicle disappear up into his body. He was now moaning regularly, but made no special sound as his semen shot out in spurts onto my hands and over his belly.

His cock had now become hypersensitive. He even winced when I touched it while wiping away the semen. Once I had dried him off, I stretched myself alongside him, we embraced and lay together for a long while. I thought, "How wonderfully affectionate he is," and once again tried to tell him without undue sentimentality, how much he meant to me. He gave only brief responses, but it was clear that he was glad to have a man he could visit and that he genuinely liked me. When he had to leave, we dressed in the semidarkness, unsure at first which underwear was whose, and then embraced several more times before he finally departed. I returned to bed and, thinking of him, brought myself to a climax.

I had learned that the next Saturday was his birthday. He would be twenty. I decided against sending him a note. "Anyway, he will go home to celebrate his birthday," I thought. But to my surprise and delight, he called Friday evening and asked to visit.

As usual he looked at the latest magazines and I showed him a book with pictures of athletes. He pointed out a young man whose body he found attractive. We were on the couch together and I lay with my head in his lap as he looked through the book. He was already aroused and soon reached down to place my hand over his cock. I massaged it through the cloth, feeling it jump at my touch. I unbuttoned his shirt   and buried my face in his woolly chest. Despite the cold weather, he was wearing no undershirt. Then I   undid his fly and drew out his cock, healthy pink, firm, beautiful. I ran my fingers over the glans. He moaned in delight. I bent further over and took it in my mouth, stroking the underside with my tongue. Again he showed his pleasure. I released his cock and moved up to kiss him on the mouth. Shortly after it was he who suggested we go to the bedroom.

Naked on the bed I buried my face in his crotch and took one testicle in my mouth. He made a sound. I, not clear if he found this pleasurable or painful, withdrew. "Shall I get the lubricant?" I asked. "Sure." Almost as soon as I spread the lubricant, he began to moan in pleasure. It was obvious that he was sexually excited. I tried to prolong his pleasure by going slowly and using a light touch, but he came soon and copiously, the first spurt hitting me on the tip of my nose, startling me, and then flooding out onto his stomach and my hand. "Happy birthday!" I said, and he had to laugh. He was surprised that I knew the date.

When the contractions subsided I wiped him dry. He helped, removing my hand from his cock, which was now painfully sensitive to touch. I now stretched alongside him and halfway over him, my leg thrown over his leg, my arm over his chest, and my head on his shoulder. We relaxed and talked. He asked, "Do you speak German?" "Yes," I answered, and explained that I had spent much time in Germany and had worked at learning the language. "Teach me three words each time I come here and I'll be able to speak German at the end of the year." I laughed. "What words do you want to know?"

"Anything. You pick something."

"How about 'ficken'?"

"What does 'ficken' mean?"

"That's German for 'to fuck'."

He laughed. "You're going to get me into trouble!"

So we practiced "Guten Morgen!" and "Wie geht's?" and I added, to myself, "Du bist schön!"

I noticed that he had twice put his hand down to his cock. I looked there and remarked, "You're getting aroused again. How can you so soon?" I did not think he would become hard, but he seemed to want my attention there. So I gently massaged it. He was indeed getting harder, and now he handed me the jar of lubricant!

I wondered if he could have another orgasm so soon, but since the first had been obviously overdue, I supposed it possible. I spread the lubricant and massaged more vigorously this time. He moaned and tossed, apparently enjoying it and straining for an orgasm. This time it took longer, but he did climax again, with a surprisingly large amount of semen. He helped me wipe it off, and laughed, "It's true what they say. It's better the second time around!" "Happy birthday, again," I replied.

He asked the time, and then rushed to leave, explaining that he had to collect his books and then join some other students. They were to celebrate his birthday at midnight. "I'll be back soon," he said. After he left, I became acutely aware of the ache in my groin. I lay on my bed and, thinking of GA, soon brought myself to climax.

GA returned a week later, looking rather rough, for he had not shaved for a couple of days. But he treated me as gently as ever. As always, I found him irresistible, and kissed and caressed him. He quickly got an erection and suggested moving from the couch to the bed. There things progressed rapidly, and with the aid of the lubricant he soon had an orgasm.

After he was cleaned up, he lay beside me. I now had an erection, so I asked him, "Will you give me an erotic massage?" He laughed, "Sure." He was a bit rough; I made several suggestions, and he tried to follow them. I sat up a couple of times to hug and kiss him. "It feels better when I do it," I thought, "but it's exciting because it is GA doing it." I came with a cry.

After I was cleaned up, we lay together again. I was expecting to enjoy the sweet lassitude in his arms. To my surprise, he took the lubricant again and spread it on himself, and without another word started to masturbate. I was astonished. Could he come again so soon?! He could, but it took a very long time of vigorous work before he again collapsed.

As we were dressing afterwards, I asked, "Do you often do it twice?" "No, not often." "You worked up a sweat." "It beats running," he joked. Our final good-nights were very tender, and he promised to visit again before going home for the Christmas holidays.

In thinking about the experience the next day, I told myself that I was happy, that I could not have expected more from him, that his sharing with me was an extraordinary bit of good fortune, completely unexpected at the age of fifty-six. And yet, this time and the week before I felt a melancholy, a deep bittersweet feeling—a wish to return to a lost youth perhaps. If I had been as open-minded as GA, I would surely have a larger store of happy memories now. But did he in fact have other friends who were sexual partners? "I wish for him someone near his age, and the two in love," I thought. I knew, too, that I would be jealous— and unhappy if it meant not seeing him. "But for his sake, I wish it were so."

I was not surprised when GA did not keep his promise to visit me before the holidays. I was surprised when he visited the second day after classes began again in January, and was astonished at his display of passion. For the first time, as we were lying together on a couch, he took off my shirt and embraced me warmly. There, and later in bed, he several times kissed me, probing deeply with his tongue. I was beside myself. "How good you are to me!" I said. But he only replied, "You're good to me."

He was early aroused, as usual. This night I, too, was already aroused before he suggested we go to bed. There he undressed down to his undershorts (and socks, which he always kept on), lay back on the bed, and when I approached said, "Take your time." I did, running my hand over his legs, up the crotch, lightly over the region of the penis, and around the edge of his shorts. He breathed in sharply, a signal of pleasure. But finally I did remove his undershorts and stretched out at length on top of him, propping myself on my knees and elbows, so as not to put all my weight on him. He embraced me tightly, kissed long and deeply, then ran his hand between us to free my penis—or place his own in a more comfortable position.

I asked if his nipples were sensitive. There were. I massaged one with a finger and ran my tongue over the other. Again he sounded his pleasure. Keeping a finger on each nipple, I slid down and took his penis in my mouth. I knew he liked that. I broke to go up for a kiss and warm embrace, then back to the penis. I kept one finger on a nipple, or ran my hand over his hairy chest —he said he liked that too—and with one hand on the base of his penis, took it firmly, deeply in my mouth. This time I could tell that he was near his climax, and soon he was moaning and coming in my mouth. I stopped all movement except swallowing.

When he had completely relaxed, I lay gently on top of him and whispered in his ear, "Happy New Year!" He laughed. Then I slid to one side and we lay for a long time in a close, warm embrace. I said, "Graham, I'm very happy." "So am I."

He announced that he had to leave. But he was in no hurry, even though—or perhaps because—he had to go back to his room and study. There were several more embraces before he finally left. I returned to my bed where, thinking of him, I brought myself to a piercing, flooding orgasm.

While walking to my office the next day I reflected on my feeling of contentment. It had, I thought, like all good things, come late in my life. But I meant to enjoy it. Odd how things had turned out—so differently from what I had originally thought. I wished I knew how GA had felt about our first meeting. How frustrated he must have felt when he was rejected, no doubt not suspecting the motive. I knew I could never ask. But I will enjoy him while he is here. And I am good to him. He knows it, and he knows he is free. One day he will leave. I won't know it because he won't say good-bye. He'll probably say, "I'll see you soon." The thought was bittersweet; but I was content.

But this time GA kept his word to "return soon" and was back eight days later. He was not so passionate, but relaxed and obviously comfortable with my show of affection. As usual, he looked through the latest magazines and I even added another book of pictures of athletes for him to look at. During this time I unbuttoned his shirt and nuzzled his warm and hairy chest and stomach. I could feel that he had an erection. I ran my hands lovingly over his chest, stopping at each nipple for a brief massage. And each time he gasped softly to show that he was enjoying it. He laid his arm around my neck while he looked through the magazine. When he finished looking at the pictures, he lay back and held me, as I continued to kiss and nuzzle him. Then he said, "Let's go to bed."

He undressed quickly, except for his undershorts, and lay on his back. I undressed entirely and, now erect myself, approached him. He said, "Take your time." I supposed he meant not to rush removing his shorts, so I ran my hand and mouth over the bulge of his cock and my finger under the crotch. Sounds from him showed this was what he wanted. But after digging out the head of his cock and kissing it, I then took off his shorts. I returned to the same spot and took his cock in my mouth, going down deeply on it several times. He showed how pleasurable he found this. I had meant to take longer to bring him to a climax, but I felt with my hand that his right testicle was drawn up, a sign that orgasm was near, so I continued the action of my mouth. He was moaning so much that I was unaware when the orgasm began, and I felt the pulsation on my lips just before the slightly salty taste of his semen. I paused until the pulsation stopped, before stretching myself over the length of him, cheek to cheek. He wrapped his arm around my back and gently caressed me. I could have stayed in that position for hours, but I knew that he would leave soon. He stayed longer than expected, but he did finally leave, again promising to return soon.

To my astonishment, GA returned two nights later, and we spent another hour and a half together, a shorter, but enjoyable, repeat of the previous visit. I was very pleased by the apparent fact that he felt completely at ease with me. I wished we had common interests to talk about, but was determined not to let such wishes spoil my enjoyment. I told him I enjoyed snuggling into the "warm fur" of his chest, but I was well aware that he was much more than a warm body for me. Since he came and went at his own choice, he must be fond of me too. Of course he expected release from his sexual tension at each visit—and seemed to have an erection from the time of his arrival—but he was also considerate of me and always gently affectionate.

I wondered if our friendship would last. Not that I thought he would deliberately break it off, but I suspected that he would be unwilling to keep in touch at a distance. His silence during my sabbatical year in Europe was proof that this was a real possibility. Yet, our relationship was more intense now, and I let myself hope that it might endure.

GA telephoned the next week, but for the first time I put him off, since I was going to a concert. He called again the following week, when I again put him off, since I was still recovering from a bad cold. I asked him to call the next evening. He said he would, but I waited in vain. Nor did I hear from him for over a month longer. My enthusiasm, affection (love?), felt on his previous visits, dissipated.

I wanted to leave him his freedom. Above all I wanted to know that his visits were completely voluntary. Finally, however, I decided to contact him, to remind him how welcome he was. I wrote a brief note and left it in his campus mailbox. He called that very evening—and the evening passed as pleasurably as before, but my feelings took a turn for the worse the following week.

The cause was this: I was in my office one morning, a college holiday, when I was surprised to see GA at my door, for I thought he would be out of town. He said that he wanted to visit, and indeed, as I was still sitting in my chair, he walked over and brushed against me to show that he already had an erection. He apparently expected to have a sexual encounter then and there. What recklessness I thought, where someone could come by and find us. The place was as inappropriate as the time was the night he visited me after midnight. But I did not want to disappoint him. My breath came fast. I said I had to work another hour, would then have lunch nearby, and go home. He asked: "When would be a good time for me to come by?"

"One o'clock?"

"OK," and he left.

Back in my house, I looked forward to his arrival. One o'clock came and went; by two o'clock I felt disappointed and frustrated; from three o'clock I sank deeper into depression, unable to work or even read. I simply brooded over the situation. "I would prefer that he never visit me," I said to myself, "than have to go through such pain." And the depression lasted for several days. No word came from GA.

The broken appointment was on the first day of a brief holiday period at the College. By the time classes resumed, I was recovering from my disappointment. GA telephoned that evening. He had profuse apologies: "I'm sorry; I really am sorry." And he had a plausible excuse: A friend who had offered to drive him home left early after hearing of sickness in his family. GA had tried to telephone before leaving, but was unable to reach me, since I was in fact out for lunch. So what could I say? I forgave him and said, "Come on over." Our love-making was perhaps not as exciting as usual, and I felt the bittersweetness of it more than ever, but—we were back together. He had probably never doubted it. How could I tell him of my doubts and fears? When he left, he promised—fervently—to visit again soon. I knew better.

But he did return only nine days later. I tried to be particularly nice to him, and he seemed very appreciative. In the bedroom, I ran my hands over his body, massaged his nipples, at which he made sounds to show he enjoyed it, and then, kneeling between his legs, I took his penis in my mouth and stayed there until he climaxed. The position had become awkward for me, so that most of his sperm dripped back onto him. He did not mind, and after standing up to wipe himself off, he lay back down on the bed and took me into his arms. I felt very good about this and snuggled against him; he held me for a long time.

But finally he did have to go. There were several parting embraces. I was very happy with the evening, so that when he promised to call again soon, I was sure he meant it. Nevertheless, I had a bittersweet feeling after his departure, because I knew our relationship was un likely to develop into anything closer. "If it were only possible to have him for a friend!" I thought. I also thought, "I do love him." I recalled something a German had once said to me: "Friendship born of love remains firm." Could it be?

It was not to be. GA did return once more, however. I knew it was our last meeting before he left for the summer recess. The visit went well, but I was more concerned that he understand that I wanted him to say good-bye to me before he left Cambridge. He promised to do this; and I wanted to believe him—and did—but as the days passed until it was impossible that he could still be on campus, my thoughts turned to acceptance of the end of our relationship. I thought it unlikely that he would contact me in the fall, when he would return for his senior year. I could not imagine now that I would respond to that unlikely event. The disappointment and frustration of those fruitless waits were too distressing.

I had to confess to myself that I did not understand him at all. It is not just callous youth, I thought. I also thought how little impression I had made on him. And I realised that I no longer desired to please him. I *had* pleased him, but now I thought even this unlikely. At any rate I no longer had the desire to try. To have that desire required believing that I meant more to him than some sort of warm masturbating machine that let him reach a climax with no effort. But his lack of concern for my feelings showed how little I really meant to him.

Two months later I tried to evaluate my experiences with him. Of course I was glad it had happened; and I knew that he had nothing to complain of. Indeed, he had always seemed appreciative. But all that was behind us. The affair was over. I had some difficulty accepting this, but was glad at the peacefulness of my life.

I saw him on campus three weeks after the beginning of the fall semester in September. I do not think he saw me. Somehow he did not look attractive; he   appeared to have gained weight. I did not look at him closely, but walked by at a distance. I wondered if perhaps my view of his appearance was prompted by my not wanting to desire him. At any rate I was sure now that, even if he asked to get together with me again, I would not. The affair with GA was in the past. I was glad it had happened, but I knew it could not be repeated. "A pity," I sighed to myself.

TEN
MEETINGS WITH
SYMONDS AND ULRICHS

PARALLEL TO MY practical experience with Alsworth was a growing interest in the theory of homosexuality. My dis cussions with Tom were very helpful, especially after Tom received from Symonds a copy of his essay *A Problem in Modern Ethics* in February 1891. Symonds had fifty copies   of his book printed, but I believe this was the only one sent across the Atlantic, which showed that Symonds must indeed have thought Tom "quite one of the most learned & clearest-headed men in the USA" as he said. Symonds was also anxious to get the opinion of "sensible people who have no sympathy with the peculiar bias." As he understood this phrase, I suppose Tom qualified, but I wondered what Symonds would think if he knew the extent of my intimacy with Tom before his marriage. At any rate, it was clear that Symonds would discount my own opinion if he knew that I was sexually active and indeed exclusively homosexual. Thus I hesitated to correspond with him directly and passed on my opinions through Tom.

The more I studied Symonds's book, however, the more irritated I became. He seemed quite determined not only to place little value on the theory of anyone known to be homo sexual, but vastly to overrate the opinions of those in the medical establishment, as if their arguments were not just as much *pro domo* as those of homosexuals! But he did give a whole chapter (which he labeled "Literature— Polemical") to the theory of Karl Heinrich Ulrichs, whose writings he became acquainted with sometime in late 1889, even though Ulrichs was himself homosexual, or—in the terminology he invented—an Urning. (Symonds used this term interchange ably with "invert," seldom using the term "homosexual," which, though linguistically mixed, was, I felt, the more neutral term.) I thought Ulrichs's theory, as presented by Symonds, vastly superior and more scientific than the other theories he discussed, but I could not agree with it either. Consequently, I wrote some of my own ideas in a letter which I gave to Tom to include with his own correspondence in May 1891. I insert the letter here.[1]

> Dear Mr. Symonds,
>
> My friend T. S. Perry will have told you that he has shared with me your fascinating *A Problem in Modern Ethics*. I wish to tell you how much I enjoyed reading it and how much I learned from it. Mr. Perry has, I believe, given you some opinions of his own on the subject. He has also encouraged me to write some of my views. Hence this letter.
>
> I will tell you first—for I think it well that you know it from the beginning—that I am personally affected by the love that you discuss in the book. Please note that I refer to love; I have not developed a theory of sexuality. I do, however, reject most decidedly the

---

[1] Most of Peirce's letter was eventually published as "Letter from Professor X." See appendix B.

theories of Krafft-Ebing and others who consider this condition some kind of nervous or mental illness. Ulrichs is surely right when he rejects that idea; I wish that you could too. But by positing a female soul in a male body Ulrichs has, in my opinion, gone astray. While that answers the question of naturalness and so avoids the taint of immorality, it does not square with the facts as I see them.

I have long considered and inquired into this question for many years; and it has long been my settled conviction that no breach of morality is involved in homosexual love; that, like every other passion, it tends, when duly understood and controlled by spiritual feeling, to the physical and moral health of the individual and the race, and that it is only its brutal perversions which are immoral. I have known many persons more or less the subjects of this passion, and I have found them a particularly high-minded, upright, refined, and (I must add) pure-minded class of men. In view of what everybody knows of the vile influence on society of the intersexual passion as it actually exists in the world, making men and woman sensual, low-minded, false, every way unprincipled and grossly selfish, and this   especially in those nations which self-righteously reject homosexual love, it seems a travesty of morality to invest the one with divine attributes and denounce the other as infamous and unnatural.

There is an error in the view that feminine love is that which is directed to a man, and masculine love that which is directed to a woman. That doctrine involves a begging of the whole question. It is a fatal concession to vulgar prejudice, and a contradiction to all you have so firmly adduced from Greek manners, and, indeed, I may say, to all the *natural* evolution of our race. Passion is in itself a blind thing. It is a furious pushing out, not with calculation or comprehension of its object, but to anything which strikes the imagination as fitted to its need. It is not characterised or differentiated by the nature of its object, but by its own nature. Its instinct is to a certain form of action or submission. But how that instinct is determined is largely accidental. Sexual passion is drawn by certain qualities which appeal to it. It may see them, or think it sees them, in a man or a woman. But it is in either case the same person. The controlling influence is a certain spiritual attraction, and that may lie in either. The two directions are equally natural to unperverted man, and the *abnormal* form of love is that which has lost the power of excitability in either the one or the other of these directions. It is *unisexual* love (a love for one sexuality) which is a perversion. The normal men love both.

It is true enough that in primitive society all passion must have been wholly or mainly animal, and spiritual progress must have been conditioned on subduing it. But there is no reason why this subjugation should have consisted in extirpating, or trying to extirpate, one of the two main forms of sexual passion, and cultivating the other. The actual reasons were, I take it, two: (1) to reserve all sexual energy for the increase of the race; (2) to get the utmost merely fleshly pleasure out of the exercise of passion. Whether either of these reasons adds to the spiritual elevation of love may be doubted. Certainly not the second, which is now the moving influence in the matter. It is true enough that all passion needs to be unceasingly watched, because the worst evils for mankind lie hidden in its undisciplined indulgence. But this is quite as true of intersexual as of homosexual love. I clearly believe that the Greek morality on this subject was far higher than ours, and truer to the spiritual nature of man; that our civilisation suffers from want of the pure and noble sentiment which they thought so useful to the state; and that we ought to think and speak of homosexual love, not as "inverted" or "abnormal," as a sort of colour-blindness of the genital sense, as a lamentable mark of inferior development, or as an unhappy fault, a "masculine body with a feminine soul," but as being in itself a natural, pure, and sound passion, as worthy of the reverence of all fine natures as the honourable devotion of husband and wife, or the ardour of bride and groom.

By the way, Professor William James appeared to have some slight insight into this when the wrote in his recent work *The Principles of Psychology* that this is "a kind of sexual appetite of which very likely most men possess the germinal possibility." I have not discussed the matter with him, however.

I trust you will not think my letter intrusive, as coming from someone acknowledged to be homosexual. By the way, Mr. Perry tells me that you are in correspondence with Ulrichs. May I ask if he still defends the theory that you described so well? And are his books still available?

Let me close by repeating my admiration for your new book. I have found it by far the best on the subject.

Sincerely yours,
James Mills Peirce.

Symonds replied before the end of May in a letter, which, not having my address, he asked Tom to convey to me. In it he assured me that I went far beyond his expectations "in hopes of regenerating opinion on these topics" and he expressed his wish that we might correspond directly. In reply to my reservations, whether he would welcome the opinion of one who was himself homosexual, he assured me that he valued and more than welcomed my "sharply-defined acute partisanship," that he had just spent some days in Siena (Symonds was then living in Davos Platz, Switzerland), where he wrote an appendix to his essay, which included new considerations that arose from the comments of the few who had read his book. Mine, he assured me, were among them. To Tom he said that he felt he had found in me "a fierce & Quixotic ally." Under the circumstances, I took that as a great compliment.

I immediately replied, thanking him for his letter and expressing my hope that we might meet to discuss the matter personally. In fact, I had already planned to spend the summer in Europe. Symonds wrote directly back, inviting me to visit him in Davos Platz; his letter reached me shortly before I sailed.

The voyage over was as smooth as my first voyage a quarter of a century before, and I was just as seasick as then. Clifford, who was again with me, was completely unaffected by the ship's motion, but was very sympathetic, returning several times a day to our cabin to see if I needed anything. I slept most of the way across the ocean; it was my best relief from my disability. Harry was very solicitous and I grew even fonder of him. Once when he felt my forehead to see if I had a fever, I turned my head slightly so that I could press my lips against his wrist. I was not sure that he had noticed, but then he said: "Does my skin feel good against your lips?" "Yes," I said. He smiled gently, caressed my cheek, and then went on with some other things he had to do. I could have hugged him tightly to me then and there— except that I did not feel the strength to even raise my arm.

A letter from Tom was waiting for me on arrival in Southampton, which cheered me greatly, as Tom's letters always did. He had crossed earlier and was then in Paris, but was to go in July to Giverny, which he and Lilla looked upon as a second (or perhaps third) home. I went to London to do some shopping and, of course, go to the opera, for Miss Eames was just then appearing in *Faust*, the very opera I had seen her in two years earlier in Paris. I thought she had improved wonderfully, and I watched the opera with deep interest. The gradual growth of passion in the Garden Scene was more real and more delicate in its intensity than I had ever seen it. The scene in the interior of the church was very powerful. The "Jewel Song" was brilliantly sung, and the whole thing a true success. The music critic Bernard Shaw agreed with me, writing "Miss Eames, as Margaret, improved on her old success." He had written of the opening of the Covent Garden Theatre season the previous April:

Faust on the following night was a very different affair. Miss Eames, the newest American soprano, fully justified her engagement by her performance as Margaret. The middle of her voice is exceptionally satisfactory in volume and rich in quality, enabling her to make herself heard without effort in all sorts of quiet dramatic inflections. The low tones, as might be expected, are also very good; but the upper register, though bright, does not come so easily as the rest; and it was rather by a *tour de force* that she took the final trio right through the third repetition in B natural instead of using the old Opéra Comique abridgment. However, as it was a successful *tour de force*, we were all very grateful for it; for the abridgment spoils the finest passage in the whole opera. As an actress, Miss Eames is intelligent, ladylike, and somewhat cold and colorless. The best that can be said for her playing the last two acts is, that she was able to devise quietly pathetic business to cover her deficiency in tragic conviction.

I believe Julian Story was in a stall box the evening I heard her but I could not very well see, as it was on my side of the house. At any rate I heard a great deal of talk about her impending marriage to the painter. It was known that they were in love and everyone knew the romantic story that he had asked her to marry him on the third time they met. Her mother opposed the marriage, however. Hence the delay. But the whole operatic world was gossiping about the possible event; and in fact they were married without her mother's consent only three weeks after I saw her in London. Apropos, it appears that the Prince of Wales,[2] who was a close friend of Miss Eames and was said to attend all her London appearances (I can testify that he was there the evening I attended), was one of the very few people "in the know" about her intention to marry Story. All very romantic.

I had earlier planned to go to Bayreuth for more opera, but Harry was not keen on the idea, so we next left for Switzerland, to visit Symonds, and then on to Florence and Rome. But first we spent a few days on the Isle of Wight. What a delightful companion Harry was—equally delightful, whether simply walking through the New Forest, the old royal hunting ground, which we spent a day doing before going to that Isle, or in the bustling cities of Italy, where we broiled from the heat. But what of that? It was glorious.

The trip through Switzerland was also enjoyable because of the spectacular scenery. I had not realised, how remote Davos is; it seemed to take forever to reach it. But it must have been the goal of many other travelers too, for when we arrived in Davos Platz we found all the hotels full. Fortunately we were able to find a room in someone's home. This is not at all uncommon there, and one has only to walk a few yards from the train station before coming across houses with "Zimmer frei" signs hanging out. After an enjoyable meal in a nearby restaurant we turned in for the night.

The next morning we breakfasted in our room and then set out to find Symonds's house. He was well known locally, so that our host could give us precise instructions to the "Haus am Hof." The house lies halfway between Davos Platz and Davos Dorf and overlooks the two villages. Standing before it, we could see to the left a nearby tree-covered mountain. There was a grand view, a bit off to the right, of

---

[2] Albert Edward (1841–1910), Prince of Wales, became King Edward VII on the death of his mother, Queen Victoria, in 1901.

snow-covered mountains in the near (and far) distance. Behind the house rose a tree-covered slope and behind it two snow-covered, rounded peaks. Although a one-family house, it is quite large, consisting of a half-basement, two floors, and a livable attic. It was painted white, with various wooden decorations. In back was a roofed walk-around.

Symonds greeted us very cordially, although it was clear immediately that his health was not good. Mrs. Symonds, too, put in a brief, but gracious appearance, and then left "the gentlemen" alone. Harry, as might have been expected, charmed Symonds, who immediately launched into a discussion of the writings of Michelangelo, whose biography he was just then preparing. Harry soon realised, however, that his presence inhibited the conversation between us from coming to the one subject that had brought me here, and he shortly after suggested that he leave the two of us alone. This he did, after arranging to meet me in the evening back at our room.

With Harry gone, Symonds quickly turned to his latest project, which he was eager to tell me about. He was just writing to the English psychologist Havelock Ellis[3] to propose a collaboration on a book to deal scientifically with the subject of homosexuality, or "Sexual Inversion," as it was referred to in the title of the eventual book. I had doubts about a collaboration with someone who, because of his medical training, would be too much inclined to stick to the neuropathic theory to explain the phenomenon, but Symonds felt that he needed somebody of medical importance to collaborate with, since if he tried to "go it alone" he would have little effect, would merely be thought an eccentric. I believe this was what he thought had happened in the case of Ulrichs, whose writings had indeed had little effect.

[3] Havelock Ellis (1859–1939). *Sexual Inversion*, the result of his collaboration with J. A. Symonds, was the first book published in his monumental *Studies in the Psychology of Sex* (7 vols., 1897–1938).

Symonds seemed confident that he could "whittle away to a mini mum" the objectionable elements in Ellis's views. My own reading of Symonds's *A Problem in Modern Ethics*, suggested to me, however, that he would be willing to grant Ellis too much, but of course I said nothing of my misgivings, not wanting to dampen his enthusiasm.

He again expressed his appreciation of my letter and asked my permission to publish parts of it as an appendix, if the project with Ellis were realised. "I shall call you there 'Professor X'," he said with a smile. Of course I agreed. He assured me that my views would be prominent, because in a separate appendix, but I rather suspected that he continued to see them as too extreme and wished them in an appendix so as not to have to discuss them on a level with other theories. He seemed to value much more the very slight concession of William James, which I had mentioned in my letter, and asked me most carefully to furnish the exact reference to it. I promised to do so. In fact, that very quotation appeared in a footnote early in the book when it was eventually published.

When I told Symonds that I found the section of Ulrichs's theory in his essay *A Problem in Modern Ethics* the most interesting, he eagerly told me about his correspondence with Ulrichs. "When I wrote that chapter," he said, "I did not know that poor Ulrichs was still alive. I have since learned that he moved to Italy in 1880 and has been living in Aquila for the past eight years. Imagine, he wrote to me first about a Latin translation of a poem of Tennyson!" Symonds laughed. "He was not aware of my interest in sexual inversion. I gave him the information he wanted and inquired discreetly, for I was not at all sure if he wished to discuss the matter, if he were still studying the subject of his earlier pamphlets. At first he was reluctant, insisting that he had taken up an entirely different cause. But it seems he could not refrain from answering my questions on the subject, and so he did discuss it after all. We have been having a quite thick correspondence. I plan to visit him in the fall, if my health allows."

Symonds then inquired if I planned to go to Italy. I told him I did, and, in fact, as he was speaking I had been reformulating my plans so as to stop in Aquila. I wished to see the valiant German for myself. Symonds then paused, a look of conspiracy come over his face, and he said to me in a somewhat lowered tone: "I think I can tell you about another project of mine. For two years I have been writing my memoirs—not a biography, but a record of my own sexual development. This will not be a case history, such as one finds in an ever increasing, already all too great abundance in the editions of Krafft-Ebing's *Psychopathia sexualis*—although, alas, it has much in common with them, I mean in the degradation and sexual misery involved—but concerns someone who has been successful in life and letters, whose opinions are valued on many subjects, and, I may honestly say, who knows how to express his feelings in a way the reader can immediately comprehend. He paused. "But when it can be published—that, my dear Peirce, is a very, very difficult question. Not in my lifetime, surely. I must trust my executor—and perhaps his executor—to exercise the correct judgment in the matter."

I expressed my appreciation of the confidence given me and agreed with him that such a project could have enormous value for the coming generation. "If only you and I had had something like that to read when we were young!" I said. Secretly, I had doubts about the real value of his project, for it there were any real progress in the matter, then by the time the work would be published, it would seem lukewarm and timid, and not at all the courageous act that Symonds thought it to be. Symonds's announcement had yet another effect on me, for I truly believe it was at that moment that I first considered writing my own memoirs, a project that must have matured over the years without my being conscious of it. I wonder whose memoirs will be published first.[4]

By then it was clear that our conversation, however interesting, was tiring poor Sym onds, and so I left, making an appointment to return the next day. In the morning, however, a note was delivered to me at breakfast saying that Symonds had taken a turn for the worse and that his doctor had forbidden all visits for at least a week. I replied with a brief note of concern for his health and my regrets that we would be unable to continue our conversation. Harry assured me that he had "done" Davos Platz in the meantime, so we packed our bags and departed for Italy.

We went directly to Florence, which, as I expected, was broiling in the summer sun, but was, as always, a glorious experience. Harry was there for the first time and I enjoyed sharing in his enthusiasm. I also enjoyed showing him the places of special interest to me and recall pointing out to him in particular the stall on the Ponte Vecchio where I had bought my lovely signet ring. He carefully looked over the wares there, thinking to purchase something like that for himself, but found nothing comparable.

From Florence we traveled to Rome, which is glorious in different ways. I could not resist pointing out to Harry a group of young lads in the Pincio who could well have been the models for the charming photographs we had seen on sale in a shop apparently frequented by 'certain' gentlemen. The photographer was identified only as "Guglielmo"; but I learned that he was, in fact, a German living

---

[4] Symonds's memoirs appeared in 1984 as *The Memoirs of John Addington Symonds*, edited and introduced by Phyllis Grosskurth (New York: Random House, 1984).

in Naples named Wilhelm von Pluschow.[5] I had already purchased several of the photographs when the shopkeeper suggested that he had others "of a more intimate nature" that might interest me. Indeed they did. And I bought several more photographs, showing the boys, not draped in ancient costumes with a Pompeiian background, as the first were, but nude and sometimes embracing. It has been my special delight to look again at those pictures on dreary nights and recall my sunny days in Rome. In fact, one day when Harry had gone out alone, I met by accident one of the boys from that day on the Pincio. He recognised me, saw my interest, and initiated a conversation. I let him do most of the talking, for my Italian was not as good as my German. But it was adequate for the occasion, and the encounter ended in a small 'adventure' back in my room. When he left, he vowed eternal friendship, as Italians do, but that did not stop him from taking the money I offered, and indeed he produced a look of disappointment that made me offer even more than I had intended. But he was worth it. He too is one of my happy memories of Rome.

Although I was anxious to go on to Aquila to see Ulrichs, I was afraid that Harry would not want to leave Rome; but the heat was so intense that he too looked forward to the higher, cooler altitude. For this very reason Aquila is a favorite summer resort of the Romans, and we had some difficulty finding a hotel on our arrival. This time Harry did not go with me, and I left him to investigate the old castle and the cathedral, while I went to the address that Symonds had given me. I found Ulrichs at home. He seemed pleased to have a visitor, especially after he learned that I had just visited Symonds, of whom he had formed a high opinion, and he was delighted to be able to

---

[5] Wilhelm von Pluschow was a cousin of the better known photographer Wilhelm von Gloeden. For a description of Pluschow's work, with illustrations, see Bruce Russell, "Wilhelm von Pluschow and Wilhelm von Gloeden: Two Photo Essays," *Visual Communications* 9, no. 2 (1983): 57–80.

speak German. Although rather sparsely furnished, his small quarters seemed crowed due to the many flower pots that were standing all about. He was obviously proud of his collection, and explained to me that many of them had been grown from seeds sent from Germany. His Turk's cap lilies were just then in bloom; he pointed out that they had the shape of glasses used to drink the sparkling wine of Champagne. His tiger-flowers were also just budding. Despite the confusion, his rooms had an altogether comfortable atmosphere. His clothes were shabby, but clean; my first impulse was one of pity for an honest and noble man who had somehow been deprived of an adequate income. But he showed not the least embarrassment, as he courteously invited me to sit at his rustic table, on which he laid our simple refreshments: some cheese and bread, summer fruit, and "in honor of the occasion" a flask of the local wine. Through the window was to be seen a wonderful view of the Gran Sasso d'Italia, whose peaks are covered in snow even in summer. I could not have enjoyed myself more at a dinner at Delmonico's!

From the newspapers that were piled up I could see that he kept up with events in Germany. He had just received the latest issue of the *Kölnische Zeitung*, in which he had read of the entry of Adolf of Nassau into Luxemburg as the Grand Duke of Luxemburg. Adolf had been duke of Nassau, but was forced to relinquish his duchy to Prussia as a result of the Prussian victory over Austria. Luxemburg was his compensation. Ulrichs showed a good deal more fire than I expected when he pointed out the statement in the paper that Germany was the best guarantee of Luxemburg's liberty. He told of Bismarck's role in the invasion and annexation of his own homeland, Hannover. The name Bismarck obviously tasted bitter on his lips. I was astonished at his strength of feeling about an event that had happened over two decades before.

I could see that he was enjoying talking about those matters, but I was determined to bring him around to discussing his Urning theory. In fact, when I made it clear that this was my main interest, he appeared only too glad to discuss it. He was very pleased to hear my opinion that Symonds had carefully reported his theory and that I had found it the best part of Symonds's book. I told him that Symonds hoped to visit him if his health would permit. Ulrichs himself, who was sixty-six years old, looked to be in the best of health. I asked him his secret. "Daily baths in the river," he said, "the Aterno." "But," I replied, "that stream is fed by melting snow. Isn't it very cold?" "Yes," he answered, with a gleam in his eye, "very cold." I told him that I preferred warm waters, and mentioned that I had visited Karlsbad because of my gallstones. He had never been there, but of course knew of the famous spa.

Ulrichs wanted to know if I agreed with his basic theory that Urning-love (he seemed to carefully avoid the term "homosexuality") is an expression of a feminine element.

"Not entirely." I tried to be diplomatic. "It appears to me that we are all basically bisexual."

"Well, some people are," he conceded, adding, almost to himself, "That is a term that Kertbeny also used." Then he continued, "But tell me about yourself. You say that you have loved men. Do you not feel like a woman toward them?"

"Not at all. I am attracted to them because they are men. But I too am a man. My attraction is of a man to a man."

"But that is just the feminine element," he countered. "It is simply feminine to be attracted to a man."

I tried to point out what I saw as a vicious circle in his argument, that he was merely begging the question, as I had written to Symonds in my first letter. But Ulrichs would not see it. He was as stubborn as he was forthright and honest. I think no one ever earned my respect so much by disagreeing with me!

I could have discussed the subject further with him, but Ulrichs announced that it was time for his afternoon walk, and invited me to join him. It was just what my body needed. We had a very pleasant walk through the town, Ulrichs pointing out the palazzo where his "good friend" the Marquis   Persichetti lived.[6] Near there we ran into Harry, who was just coming from a visit to the cathedral, and I introduced the two. Ulrichs was again delighted to find someone who spoke German, and he was charmed by Harry, whom he obviously found attractive. The three of us then stopped in a café. I think the elegant proprietor was a bit offended by Ulrichs's rather shabby appearance—he muttered something about "crazy Germans"—but Ulrichs did not let it disturb him. Nor did Harry, although I think he too found Ulrichs somewhat eccentric. When I paid our waiter, Ulrichs graciously thanked me. Outside, we said our good-byes. Ulrichs wanted to stop by a newsstand before going home; Harry had found a curious souvenir shop he wanted to show me.

There was indeed much to see in Aquila, but when we left the next morning I felt that I had seen the principal thing there. I formed a tremendous admiration for Ulrichs. He had fought a noble fight, had been betrayed even by those who should have supported him, and yet had survived with a great sense of self-worth. No doubt he was a man "ahead of his time"; I could only hope that future generations would come to appreciate the greatness of the man. I can truly say that meeting him is one of the experiences I cherish most in my memory.

[6] Niccolò Persichetti (1849–1915), archaeologist and historian, published a memorial booklet in honor of Ulrichs a year after his death.

ELEVEN
SEXUAL INVERSION

THE SUMMER HAD passed all too quickly. I did not have a chance to visit Tom and Lilla in Giverny, but I knew they would return to Boston in the fall. Harry was one of the reasons why the time went by so, for he was an ideal traveling companion. I regret very much that he was never able to return to Europe with me, but we remained good friends, although I have hardly seen him since his marriage in the summer of 1896.

The beginning of the fall semester was a busy time for me, more with administrative duties than with teaching, so that I saw little of Tom on his return to Boston in November. But by the beginning of 1892 we were together more often than at any time since his marriage. I had persuaded him to join me in the St. Botolph Club,[1] and evening after evening found us there, if not for dinner, at least for cards, cigars, and lively conversation. At the beginning of February Tom showed me a letter he was writing to his friend (and former student) Leonard Opdycke about being a new member of the Club:

---

[1] The St. Botolph Club in Boston was founded in 1880, on the model of the New York Century Club, by William Dean Howells, Francis Parkman, and others.

I have nothing more to do with my once happy home; it is deserted; the fire is never lit in my library; I scarcely know my children by sight. I spend all my time here wildly revelling. . . .

We are a wild set; J. M. Peirce & I especially sit up to midnight &, as it were, personally lead the dance.

Although Tom used a joking tone here, it was not far from the truth, for we really were together often, and I sometimes wondered what Lilla thought of all this. But she did not complain, certainly not to me, and I suspect she was rather glad not to have him constantly in the house. For my part, I had never felt so content. True, I was not experiencing "heights of passion" or other such excitements; but neither was I in depths of depression, or with bouts of self-doubt, or concern about career choices, and all the other things that had disturbed me earlier. My life was calm and serene. I was nearly 58 years old and happy with myself. I did think I had contributions to make—to sexual progress, perhaps, and to mathematics—but the need was not pressing.

I continued to enjoy what Boston had to offer in the way of theatre and, especially, music. Miss Eames had opened the winter season at the Metropolitan Opera in New York, and came to Boston this year in a triumphal return. One of her European critics had said that her cool delivery as Aida was like "skating on the Nile," but coldness is a New England trait, and the Bostonians appreciated her ladylike composure. I thought her voice near perfection.

The saddest event of 1892 was the death at age thirty-three of Tom's intimate friend and former student George Pellew, a really promising poet. Tom was persuaded to edit a selection of his poems, which was published that same year. Knowing his intimacy with Pellew, William James asked Tom in April, shortly after his death, to take part in a sitting with Leonora Piper in James's home, in an attempt to communicate with Pellew. Tom really had little faith in the possibility, but as I had already planned to attend, he went with me. Many present were convinced that Mrs. Piper was indeed in contact with Pel lew, but, alas, nothing informative resulted from this 'contact' and no further attempts were made.

Mrs. Piper had appeared on the scene in 1884 and in the beginning did not seem to differ from the ordinary American trance medium. The following year, however, James was attracted to her and she has since been under the supervision of the Society for Psychical Research, which was founded in Boston in 1885, with Simon Newcomb, the astronomer, as president. James persuaded me and Alexander Graham Bell, among others, to also be founders of the Society, but I have never shared his enthusiasm for psychical research; and I fear that his own interest has harmed his reputation as a psychologist. As for Mrs. Piper, she appears to be absolutely honest and the validity of her trances is difficult to deny. After an initial period in which she spoke in the voice of her control, whom she identified as a French physician called "Dr. Phinuit," she had in 1892 already begun the automatic writing by a "control" known as "George Pelham," the pseudonym of a young American author. Perhaps it was the similarity of that name to "George Pellew" that made the group in attendance in April so optimistic.

The following year everyone talked about the International Exhibition in Chicago. Tom went, and returned glowing reports, but I did not go. I think I was the only one of my acquaintances who did not! That was also the year of the first American translation of Krafft-Ebings's infamous *Psychopathia sexualis*. It was a translation of the seventh German edition, which shows what a best-seller the book had already become since its original publication in 1886. How I detested that book and especially his treatment of the noble Ulrichs in it. He nearly insists that Ulrichs himself was pathological and calls his explanation "superficial." And I longed for the promised book by Ellis and Symonds. But Symonds's death on April 19, 1893, delayed completion of the book for several years (and then there was all the difficulty of finding a publisher).

The musical delight of the year was the arrival of the Metropolitan Opera in Boston in the fall of 1893, before opening the season in New York. Miss Eames had hurt herself on the train and sang the Countess in *Le Nozze di Figaro* with her arm in a sling—and sang as well as I have ever heard her. The very next day she was Marguerite, bringing to Boston her Paris and London success.

In the spring of 1894 there was a theatre novelty at Harvard when Professor Allen (who had collaborated with Professor Greenough on an excellent Latin grammar) directed a full-scale production of the comedy *Phormio* of the Roman playwright Terence on April 19. Not only was the entire comedy presented in Latin, but the program and even the tickets were printed in Latin. I sent copies of both to Ulrichs, knowing he would be interested; he replied with profuse thanks—in Latin, of course. My own Latin was good enough to read his letter, but hardly adequate for an answer. Thus I let any further correspondence drop. The following year I learned that he had died. His friend, the Marquis Persichetti had him buried next to his own family tomb; at the funeral he praised   Ulrichs as a lover of the Latin language. One day, perhaps, he will be praised as a lover of his fellow men, a fighter for sexual liberation, a pioneer of the Urning cause. I believe his name and theory are again being discussed in interested circles in Berlin.

April was a sad month for me: Tom left for an extended stay in Europe, and indeed was away three years. But I too went to Europe in the summer and was able to see Tom in Paris, to which he made occasional trips from Giverny, where he was spending the summer months. To my delight, my brother Bert had been appointed by President Cleveland to be secretary of the U.S. Legation at St. Petersburg in May. I planned to visit him there that summer, but again felt the need to return to Karlsbad and had to give up the possibility of a visit to Russia. In fact, my return to Cambridge was delayed as I left Europe later than expected, sailing from Southampton only at the end of October.

My delight in the progress of Bert was countered by my relations with my brother Charles, which again deteriorated during that year. His financial situation had worsened since he was forced to resign from the Coast Survey at the beginning of 1891. Typically, he refused to accept responsibility for his situation and placed all blame on the ill will of others. For example, when he was not allowed to take with him the books he had been using, since they were bought with government funds, he remarked: "The dirty fellows who played this trick got nothing by it except the pleasure of harming me."

Now he was projecting the writing of textbooks in arithmetic and geometry, which he had no doubt would bring in a large income. But in the meantime, of course, he needed a cash advance, which his publisher—for good financial reasons—refused to grant. Naturally he turned to me; I knew it would be useless to give him a substantial sum, for he would only squander it, but I began to send him small amounts occasionally. Far from being grateful, he began to complain that I was letting him starve!

His publisher, apparently in an attempt to bring their negotiations with him to some kind of resolution, suggested that they would be receptive to a collaboration with me. Charles proposed this to me, writing to me in November about his own treatment of geometry: "I think my work is in the spirit which father always radiated; although I admit that I have not been able to attain his classical simplicity. If you would take the hold of it, I believe you would do a good deal toward that. It is in some aspects like a book you always, I thought, underrated, JMP's Analytical Geometry." But I saw through his flattery and declined the cooperation. I knew that the result would have been a great deal of work on my part, only to be frustrated by his criticisms and insistence that everything be done his way. Of course he put this down to ill will on my part, and continued his complaints. In the end nothing came of that publishing project—one that he could easily have completed, if he had been more practical and a bit more ready to compromise with his publisher.

By January 1895 it appeared that Charles's poor handling of his financial situation had led to his being threatened with a criminal prosecution. I advised him to obtain good legal advice, but apparently he thought the situation beyond such practical measures. He replied with phrases such as: "I am very ill," "Juliette has left me," "I cannot now prevent a sheriff's sale or worse," "I have to crawl into a corner & die." There was nothing to do but go to Pennsylvania and see for myself. This I did, and found Charles in a pitiful state. It was not entirely true that Juliette had left him, but she was ill herself, more so than he was, I think, but his situation was bad. I spent a good deal more money on him than I had meant to—and carefully avoided any expressions of disapproval, though I did urge him to be more realistic in financial matters.

I could not stay away from Cambridge long and soon returned, but a letter Charles wrote in mid-February reassured me that he was on the road to recovery. He said he had given up thoughts of suicide, was determined to make money and pay off his debts, etc. I would have been willing to help him with larger sums to pay off those debts, if I had thought that he would not immediately incur new ones, but by now I knew better. I continued to send small amounts when they appeared to be really needed. The result was that he would thank me for the "little cheque"—and immediately ask for more.

Near the end of June 1895 I left for Europe, going first to London. My principal goal was to visit Bert in St. Petersburg, a visit postponed from the year before, but on the way I stopped again at Karlsbad, for I had been ill in May, apparently with my old gallstones. In Karlsbad I stayed at my former hotel, and was greeted like an old friend. By the end of August, however, I was in St. Petersburg, where I had a most enjoyable visit with Bert, so very different from my last visit to our brother Charles! When he was younger we had all despaired of Bert because of his poor performance as a student. Thus it was all the more gratifying to see him doing so well. The city itself is fascinating, with much to offer in the way of theatre and music. Bert knew my tastes and arranged many such evenings. The food was much better than I had expected. I remember writing to Tom from Moscow, which I visited in Bert's company, about the delicious caviar.

My return to Cambridge in September found me in a new administrative position: Dean of the Faculty of Arts and Sciences. (Professor John H. Wright became Dean of the Graduate School.) Eliot said he needed my "diplomatic" skills more in the new position; I told him that I had just visited my diplomat-brother and had learned much in that line. Indeed I needed all my skills in that position, for there were always disagreements between faculty and students on the application of various rules, which I was called upon to adjudicate. Fortunately the simple letter-press method of copying typewritten letters allowed me to keep a complete record of correspondence from my office, which helped resolve many disagreements.

By the following year I was beginning to believe that, following Symonds's death, Ellis must have given up the idea of publishing *Sexual Inversion*, the planned title of his collaboration with Symonds. Thus I was not a little surprised when I learned of a German translation[2] published in 1896. William James called my attention to it. He knew that I had visited Symonds in Switzerland and probably suspected that I had more than a passing interest in the subject. The book had been received by the journal *Psychological Reviews* and assigned to William Noyes at the Boston Insane Hospital in Mattapan to review, but before passing it on. James had read and formed an unexpectedly favourable opinion of it. He was especially pleased to see a quotation from his *Principles of Psychology* in it. According to James's report to me later, Noyes found the book "distasteful" and "repugnant." As the publication of the English version in 1897 has been largely ignored, his review, which was not published until the following year, may be inserted here to show the reception that the work generally received.

> It would not be right not to enter a protest against the appearance of such a work as this in a library intended primarily for popular reading. Even Krafft-Ebing, although writing solely for the medical profession, has been severely and justly criticised for the unnecessary emphasis and importance he has given this subject

---

[2] Havelock Ellis and J. A. Symonds, *Das konträre Geschlechtsgefühl*, trans. Hans Kurella, Bibliothek für Socialwissenschaft mit besonderer Rücksicht auf sociale Anthropologie und Pathologie, vol. 7 (Leipzig: Georg H. Wigand's Verlag, 1896).

by his articles on the perversions of the sexual sense, and nothing but harm can follow if popular scientific literature is to suffer a similar deluge. Medical literature of the last few years contains altogether too many histories of these unfortunate individuals who have only discovered themselves to be abnormally afflicted after reading a description of their condition in one of the many monographs or medical journal articles, and the alienist has come to look regularly for a series of sexual pervert autobiographies after the appearance of each new monograph.

If an intelligent understanding of his condition could ever lead to an amelioration of it we might endeavour to endure in silence, but his attention invariably returns to his case and the sexual pervert merely establishes a bond of sympathy between himself and his fellow sufferers; and the world is the worse off in that the sum of morbid introspection has been increased without any corresponding gain whatever. Apart from its influence on the perverts themselves no healthy person can read this literature without a lower opinion of human nature, and this result in itself should bid any writer pause. The writers of the present volume have done their work well, from their point of view, and have threshed over the literature most thoroughly from Bible time down adding three hundred more pages to a literature already too flourishing.[3]

---

[3] William Noyes, review of *Das konträre Geschlechtsgefühl*, by Havelock Ellis and J. A. Symonds, *Psychological Reviews* 4 (1897): 447.

After James had mentioned to me that the book was to be reviewed, I regularly checked each issue of *Psychological Reviews*, wondering if my "Professor X" letter to Symonds would be mentioned. When I finally read the review, I was infuriated, not that my letter was not mentioned, but that *nothing* in the book was mentioned. The reviewer was sorry that it had been written and was apparently determined to keep everyone in ignorance of its contents. I have seldom seen such a superficial 'review.' Where was the vaunted enlightenment of our scientific age! Certainly not among the practicing psychol ogists of the medical profession. I wondered if the reviewer had even read the book; he could easily have written his empty review without doing so.

By the time I read that review, I had already received a copy of the publication in English. Along with a copy of my letter to him, Symonds had sent Ellis a note saying that I was to receive a copy of the published work. Thus it was that Ellis sent me a copy directly on publication; with it was a letter explaining that the delay was due to the difficulty in finding an English publisher; hence the German translation had appeared earlier. I had by then also already read the German version, for James had got the copy back from Noyes and lent it to me. Thus I could put the new English version into my library without cutting the pages.

As an aside, let me express my pleasure that the German edition was printed with Roman letters. I hope this trend will continue. It is much easier to read than books printed with Gothic letters, which Tom once called "the most crabbed exaggeration of the monkish perversion of Latin letters." I always thought it regrettable that Prince Bismarck encouraged their use; perhaps his resignation signaled a change.[4]

---

[4] Otto Eduard Leopold von Bismarck (1815–1898) became first chancellor of the new German Empire in 1870; he resigned in 1890. The use of Gothic type, called *Fraktur* in Germany, gained new popularity there in the wave of nationalism preceding World War I.

I have now nearly brought my story up to date. I have only to add Tom's departure in April. I am sure I shall miss him dreadfully. President Eliot recommended him for a position as professor of English literature at Keiogijuku University in Japan. I was astonished when Tom accepted the three-year appointment; that is almost the longest he has ever been in one place. I wonder if he will stay that long. Indeed, I wonder what sort of reception he will have in Japan, where they surely have mixed emotions about his great-uncle Commodore Perry, who opened up Japan to contact with western powers in 1854. But I will close my "memoirs" for now. It is appropriate to do so on my sixty-fourth birthday.

James Mills Peirce
    May 1, 1898

TWELVE
JOHN HENRY MACKAY

IT HAS BEEN over seven years since I left off my memoirs. I intended to add to them regularly, but now it is November 1905 and I have written nothing in the meanwhile. Tom's departure for Europe last month has put me in a blue mood. I am seventy-one years old and have a strong premonition that I shall never see him again. But I could be mistaken: I nearly had the same impression when he left for Japan. Tom himself was surprisingly enthusiastic about his stay in Japan at first. Later his letters revealed a homesickness for Boston, and indeed, after returning, he stayed here more than four years. They were good years for me. Our closeness immediately returned and I saw him often, both at the St. Botolph Club and in my home, where he was a frequent dinner guest.

I plan to retire in March of 1907, when I shall have completed fifty years of service to Harvard University. I am satisfied that I have been a good teacher and I have received recognition, from Eliot at least, that I have contributed significantly as an administrator. And finally, to my own great satisfaction, I think I have made a small mark as a creative mathematician. I am astonished that this has come so late in my career;

it has always been one of my goals. But let me go back now and pick up the chronology of my memoirs.

It was the First International Congress of Mathematicians in Zurich in August 1897 that revived my determination to do something noticeable in mathematics. I did not go, but I received a glowing report from William Osgood,[1] who represented Harvard there. He was particularly impressed by the size and ability of the Italian delegation, which included Giuseppe Peano, one of the principal speakers of the congress. I planned a sabbatical leave from the university for the following year, which I meant to spend in Eu rope, of course. There I wanted to meet Peano and other mathematicians whom I had heard about. Shortly before sailing in October 1898 I finally joined the American Mathe matical Society as evidence of my new seriousness as a "creative mathematician."

The American Legation in St. Petersburg having been raised to the rank of an Embassy, my brother Bert was appointed First Secretary of Embassy that year. I wanted to visit him there again. Thus I was particularly looking forward to the year. But I almost did not get away, for shortly before I was to leave, Juliette telegrammed me that Charles was sick. I considered whether I should go to him as she expected, but in the end decided that it was another of his exaggerations and was probably not serious, and so I sailed any way. (As it turned out, I was right to do so.)

My ship landed in Birmingham, from where I proceeded directly to London, to enjoy a round of theatre, then on to Paris for more of the same. But winter was coming and I wished to enjoy some of the warmth of the south of Italy. First, however, I went to Turin in hopes of meeting Peano. I had not been to Turin before and was astonished to find how much it resembles Paris with its elegant shops and well-laid-

---

[1] William Fogg Osgood (1864–1943) was professor of mathematics at Harvard (1903–1933).

out streets, not at all like the meandering inner-city streets of Milan and Rome. As good luck would have it, I found Peano in his office at the university—and he found time for me, although, as he explained to me, he was very busy with his numerous projects.

Peano is a lively man, not good looking, but quite charming. After some initial fumbling in Italian, we settled on speaking French, since I was rather more proficient in it than in Italian, and Peano himself was fluent. There was a mix-up at first, because he thought I was Charles, whose name he knew, but we soon cleared that up. He then asked about my mathematical interest. When I told him "quaternions," his eyes lit up. "But then you must be a member of the International Association which was organised last year!" he exclaimed. I was indeed. He too was a member—and thus we found our common interest. But he mostly talked about how the printing press he bought earlier in the year was helping him to present his ideas in logic and mathematics. "It is the same press that was used by my saintly old teacher Faà di Bruno[2] to print some of his works," he told me. "This, for example." He held up a copy of Faà di Bruno's *Formes Binaires* of 1876.

Peano explained that Faà di Bruno was ordained a priest that same year (1876), that he had earlier founded a home for poor girls, and had the novel idea that they could become excellent typesetters. Thus he installed the printing press there. The press had hardly been used for the past ten years since his death, and when Peano had the press moved several copies of *Formes Binaires* were found hidden behind it. "So I can give you one," he said. I accepted it gratefully. He then invited me to a nearby café for ice cream, where we continued our conversation.

By the time we left the café Peano was treating me like an old

---

[2] Francesco Faà di Bruno (1825–1888). After a brief career as a military officer, Faà di Bruno studied mathematics in Paris under Cauchy and then in Turin, where he became a professor in 1871. He was beatified by Pope John Paul II on 25 September 1988.

friend. He wrapped his arm affectionately around mine as we strolled along the elegant arcades. The weather was chilly, but it was a memorable visit and I was very glad that I had gone out of my way to Turin. Peano's encouragement meant much to me in my study of quaternions when I returned to Harvard the following year. I was awed, however, by what he had accomplished in mathematics. After all, he was twenty-five years younger than I—a quite extraordinary man! He invited me to accompany him two weeks later to a meeting of the local organisation for school teachers, in which he took a great interest; they were to discuss the proper method of introducing irrational numbers in the classroom. But I did not stay; I was anxious to go on south, to a warmer climate.

In fact, I went directly past Rome and stopped at the highest point of the railway between Naples and Salerno at the picturesque town of Cava dei Tirreni. One of Tom's friends had recommended it to me. It was a favourite resort of the Neapolitans in the summer, but during the remainder of the year most of the visitors were foreign. I stayed at a guest house that had been installed in an ancient Norman tower, and it was there that I met one of the most interesting characters of my life: John Henry Mackay.[3]

[The following is from Peirce's notebook.]

John Henry Mackay

Despite his Scottish name, Mackay was German. He was only in his mid-thirties, but already balding and

[3] John Henry Mackay (1864–1933), lyric poet and anarchist propagandist. The son of a Scottish marine insurance broker, who died when Mackay was nineteen months old, he returned with his mother to her native Germany, where he grew up. Mackay also wrote novels and short stories, and from 1905 waged an underground literary campaign for the cause of man-boy love.

beginning to be stout. Yet he carried himself with such sureness and grace that one could only think of him as a "gentleman." Beyond the customary greetings at meals, we hardly spoke at first, for he seemed to value his privacy and, at any rate, took great care not to intrude into the privacy of others. Thus it was some time before I was able to connect him with the author of *The Anarchists*, which had been published in Boston some years earlier. I had not read it. Tom had, of course, and reported to me that it attempted to justify the anarchists who had caused such trouble in Chicago in 1886. Tom did not approve of anarchists; but his report was much too superficial, as I soon learned, and I was sorry that I had not read the book.

Certainly Mackay himself appeared to be the exact opposite of the wild, bomb-throw ing fanatic that the newspapers had pictured all anarchists at that time. He was one of the most gentle persons I have ever known, especially with the young lads who seemed to be instinctively drawn to him. For he could hardly finish his breakfast before one or two of the local boys, age about fourteen, were standing by his table chatting with him. The woman who served breakfast wanted to chase them away, but Mackay insisted they be allowed to stay. He would pat them on the head, hold a hand to inspect scratched fingers when they told of their misadventures, and in general had a charming way of dealing with them. I was fascinated by this interest and determined to speak to him.

I found some kind of excuse, so as not to seem to intrude, and managed to strike up a conversation. Once the contact was established, it continued. He was in fact a very sociable man; it was only the 'anarchist' shell of privacy that was difficult to break through. Since I began the conversation, I naturally spoke German. But I quickly found out that his English was quite good, and thereafter we spoke only in English. He had visited the United States five years earlier and enjoyed reminiscing about his trip, which had also included Boston. I got an entirely different view of the Haymarket affair from Mackay, who had visited the cemetery where the "martyrs" were buried and had written a poem there to commemorate them. His book *The Anarchists* includes a whole chapter on "The Tragedy of Chicago."

Mackay told me that he was resting up from a very busy year. In 1898 he published his biography of Max Stirner, the philosopher of egoism, which he had been preparing for many years; Mackay insisted that it was he who first saw the anarchist elements in Stirner. He had also edited a collection of Stirner's minor writings. And he had published a collected edition of his own lyric poetry.

"Are you writing anything now?" I asked. We were seated at a small table on the terrace enjoying an after-lunch coffee. The view was gorgeous; we could see both bays below us in the distance. The terrace itself was covered with a magnificent display of brilliant red bougainvillea.

"I have just completed a short story," he replied. "It is very brief, nothing very important." He paused a moment and then added, "Would you care to read it?"

I told him I would, and he fished a manuscript from his case and handed it to me. "I will be very interested in your comments," he said. "But now I'm afraid I have to leave you. I have an appointment with"—a slight pause—"someone."

"Of course," I said, and he left. The way he had said "someone" gave me pause. I rather suspected he meant to see one of the boys who had spoken to him at breakfast—but why the discreet "someone"?

The story was indeed very brief, but it took me some time to read it, for his handwriting was horrible. I translated the title as "A Farewell: A Late Letter."[4] It was a "framework" story: In the "frame" a great writer has just died and his wife is going through the mail that   arrived for him after his death. But the core of the story is the content of one of the letters, which is apparently from someone who loved him in his youth and who now recalls that love late in life. Returning to the "frame": The widow tears up the letter, glad that her husband did not live to read it. There were curious elements in the story, and not the least curious was the fact that Mackay had dated it: Sorrento 1898. If he had "just finished" it, why not "Cava dei Tirreni"?

[4] Mackay's "Ein Abschied: Ein später Brief" was included in his *Gesammelte Werke*, 8 vols. (Berlin-Treptow: Verlag B. Zack, 1911). It was most recently reprinted in John Henry Mackay, *Zwischen den Zielen* (Freiburg/Br.: Verlag der Mackay Gesellschaft, 1984), pp. 95–98; in English as "A Farewell: A Late Letter," *Paidika: The Journal of Paedophilia* 2, no. 3 (1991): 48–49.

I did not see him again until the next morning, when I joined him at breakfast. I returned his manuscript, telling him that I had much enjoyed reading it. He seemed pleased—and expectant, apparently waiting for my comments.

"There were two things I found rather curious," I began. "I wonder that you never state in any way the sex of the writer of the letter." At this, Mackay searched my face, as if he had not at all expected me to notice this. "And I wonder why you dated it 'Sorrento'." At this, he blushed quite red, so much so that I felt I must have touched on something very private. In my embarrassment I was unable to excuse myself. Mackay recovered first and reassured me.

"I am only amazed," he said, "that you noticed. I would very much like to discuss this with you." And he again searched my face, as if to try to detect the extent of my interest. Apparently satisfied, he said, "Perhaps we could discuss it while walking. Would you care to join me on a visit to the abbey near here? I'm told it is worth seeing."

It was a beautiful day for a walk, and the Benedictine abbey of La Trinità della Cava was indeed worth seeing. It was an ancient abbey, built on a hill to the south-west in the village of Corpo di Cava, and although not far away required a bit of a climb. (Why are religious shrines always built on high places that are difficult to reach?) But we walked slowly; Mackay seemed careful to take my age into account, and at any rate we were in no hurry.

We were hardly on our way when Mackay inquired about my reaction to his short story. "You know, Mister Peirce, most readers will simply assume that the writer of the letter in the story is a woman and never notice that I have nowhere indicated if it is a man or a woman. And yet, I confess to you, I did take care not to say which—and that is not easy to do in German. It is somewhat easier in English, I think." He laughed somewhat nervously. "You are perceptive indeed to have noticed it."[5]

I decided at this point that, if the conversation was to continue at a realistic level, I would have to be totally honest. "I have long been alert to such indications," I said. "You see, I myself am a lover of men, and I know that many writers make a character in a story a woman, when they really have a man in mind. How I wish such writers could be more honest! Yet I know how unaccepting the world is; it does not understand how natural, how really noble such a love can be."

My comment, though no doubt not entirely unexpected, was yet so strong that Mackay paused briefly in his walking and looked at me, his mouth slightly open. Then his eyes lit up. "My dear Mister Peirce, how delighted I am to hear you say such things! Yes indeed, you are quite right. I had a man in mind when I wrote that story. And not just a fictional man

[5] Peirce was indeed perceptive: Neither Mackay's American nor his German biographer pointed this out, and even the usually astute Edward Mornin, in his literary study *Kunst und Anarchismus: "innere Zusammenhänge" in den Schriften John Henry Mackays* (Freiburg/Br.: Verlag der Mackay Gesellschaft, 1983), assumed that the writer of the letter was a woman.

but a real man. So I could not bring myself to make the character a woman. But I did not dare write everything. To leave out the sex of the person was my solution. I knew most readers would not see beyond the conventional—and could still enjoy the story— while a select few could, without contradiction, picture the character to themselves as a man—and enjoy the story even more that way." He walked on, but stopped again. "You did enjoy it?"

"I did indeed." We resumed walking. "And I in turn am delighted that my being a lover of men does not disturb you."

"Not at all. I know many such men." Now was the time when I would expect him to enlighten me about himself, but he did not. I wondered why not.

"I am curious about one other thing in the story," I said. "The ages of the two lovers are vague. It is clear that the writer of the letter is quite old, but you really do not indicate how old the woman's husband was at the time of his death. I suppose that he was not very old. That seems to indicate that there was a difference in the ages of the two lovers, does it not?"

"Yes, that is true."

"Could he have been still a boy?" I guessed.

Again Mackay paused. "You are very, very perceptive. The writer of the letter is an aging lover of boys."

It was all becoming clear to me: the boys at breakfast, his interest in them, their obvious fondness for him. I had to know. "The boys here seem to be very fond of you," I said.

He could have taken this as a change of subject, but he was too honest. "Well, you have guessed it. You told me that you are a lover of men; I will tell you that I am a lover of boys. I have lived the experience described in the letter; the letter itself is how I think—I hope—I will feel about the experience when I am old."

"And that is why you could not bring yourself to make the character a woman, because it is you."

"Exactly. You see, there is a movement in Berlin, where I am now living, to gain more acceptance for homosexuals, and they have based their ideas on the premise that a lover of men is somehow feminine. I myself see nothing of the feminine in me. I never think of myself as a woman. Hence I could not even disguise myself in the story as a woman."

"You must feel very strongly about the matter."

"Indeed I do, and I will tell you more about it, but first I wonder if you have now also guessed why I dated the story 'Sorrento'."

"I suppose you were inspired to write it while on a visit there. It is not far away." I looked in the direction of Sorrento, which was, however, hidden from sight.

"Right again," said Mackay. "The boy was someone I met on a previous visit when I stayed in Sorrento. I had hoped to find him again, but when I returned I learned that he was in love with a girl. He had nearly forgotten me. I thought it best to leave, and so I came here to this lovely spot"—he waved his arm—"and wrote the story to put my own ending to the affair."

"Now I understand," I said.

We had reached the abbey by then. The abbot had seen us coming and was waiting for us at the entrance. He was a very friendly man, genuinely proud of the beauties of the church and especially the old Gothic cloisters, which were preserved. It was an ancient abbey, nearly 900 years old, but the church, which contained several interesting sarcophagi and a fine organ, had been modernised near the end of the eighteenth century. When we entered, the Benedictine monks of the abbey were just then singing Sext, so we stopped to listen, and the abbot went to join them.

As we were leaving the church the abbot suddenly popped up again with the suggestion that he show us the valuable documents kept in the abbey. We declined the offer, and in turn offered the abbot a sum of money for his trouble. He did not decline our offer; he thanked us very graciously and offered to pray for our souls.

When we were out of earshot, Mackay said with a laugh, "Much good may his prayers do him! If he knew what an atheist I am he would not bother to pray—or perhaps he would pray all the harder." He looked at me.

"I do not share his faith either." I paused, then added, "though I was quite religious in my youth."

"Ah, well let us not talk about such useless things. I want to hear your ideas on our earlier topic, for I see that you must have given the subject of homosexuality much thought."

"I have," I agreed. "I have even been published on the subject—in English and in German." I smiled.

"I have read most of the recent books on the subject in German." Mackay looked puzzled. "I do not recall your name."

"I should be more modest," I replied. "Only a letter from me to John Addington Sym onds was published in a book by him and Havelock Ellis, and my name was not even on the letter. It was from a 'Professor X'."

"I know the book," Mackay interrupted. "I read it two years ago. I thought your letter the only really sensible thing in the book." He seemed pleased with his judgment. "Too much space was given to the medical theories of Krafft-Ebing and others like him. What do they know?!"

"But I thought the discussion of Ulrichs's theory was presented thoroughly and impartially, and it really is a positive theory."

"I have a tremendous admiration for the courage of that man, and of course his theory was progressive—for the time. After all, it did allow him to speak out for his fellow Urnings"—he said the word with some distaste —"but it simply does not square with the facts. And in the end it did not gain him the goal he desired; it only prompted the medicine men to cook up their outrageous brew of sickness and madness. Where did it get Ulrichs?"

"I have to agree with you. Yet, when I spoke with him in Aquila a few years ago, he still stubbornly held to his theory."

"Ulrichs is alive, in Italy?!" He seemed quite startled.

"Alas, no longer. He died three years ago."

"I wondered what happened to him." He was silent for a moment. "But I do not think the problem of society's intolerance can be solved with theories—not even true ones. It seems to me that the viewpoint of anarchism offers the only practical solution. That is, a realisation that, if we are ever going to live together peacefully on this world we must stop trying to impose our individual views on others, stop trying to tell them how to lead their lives. Everyone's life is his own; let him live it as he will." He saw my questioning look. "As long, of course, as he does not harm others or interfere in their lives more than they interfere in his."

"But I wonder," I couldn't help asking, "if you do not believe my view of the essential bisexual nature of human beings to be correct?"

"I have no doubt about it," he replied. "But it is not how most of us—most people—*feel* about ourselves. The intolerance of society stunts the growth of the individual. Thus, rather than try to persuade people that ours is the correct theory, I think it more important, more practical to persuade them to allow the individual to develop in his own way. If that is done—and your theory really is true—then the individual will simply develop that way, and he will 'evidence' your theory."

"Yes, I see what you mean," I replied. "But I must think about these matters further. And I will read your book about anarchism when I return to Boston," I promised.

Mackay seemed eager to add to my reading list. "And since you do read German, let me recommend Max Stirner's book *Der Einzige und sein Eigentum*.[6] Do you know it?"

"Not yet." I tried to be diplomatic.

My diplomacy was not needed, for Mackay was very pleased to be able to alert me to the value of Stirner. In fact, for the remainder of our conversation the topic of homosexuality was entirely dropped as he expounded for me Stirner's philosophy of egoism.

---

[6] An excellent English translation of this work appeared in 1907. For a more recent reprint, see Max Stirner, *The Ego and His Own*, translated by Steven T. Byington, edited, with annotations and an introduction, by James J. Martin (New York: Libertarian Book Club, 1963).

THIRTEEN
CAVIAR AND OTHER
RUSSIAN DELIGHTS

I GREATLY ENJOYED my conversations with Mackay and regretted having to leave. But having stored up as much as I could of the wonderful warmth of Italy, I left for the cold of Russia, to visit my brother Bert in St. Petersburg. And I returned to the world of math ematics, for even before leaving Cambridge I had begun considering the connection between linear equations of quaternions and determinants of quaternions. I did not think anyone had dealt with such determinants before; it seemed to furnish a topic for me to bring before the American Mathematical Society. As a new member, I felt the need to present something. I began writing my paper already on the train to Russia, completed it in St. Petersburg in January 1899, and sent it to my colleague (and former student) Professor Maxime Bôcher to read at the next meeting of the Society in February. I fear the paper was not well received. Poor Bôcher had to take the brunt of the criticism. The outcome was that the paper was never published; only an abstract appeared.[1]

Russia was indeed a change from Italy! But my brother made everything so comfortable for me that I did not mind the cold as much as I expected. In the end I stayed over two months, much longer than

---

[1] "Determinants of Quaternions." See appendix B.

I had originally planned. My greatest interest was to observe with my own eyes the regard and consideration in which Bert was held there in diplomatic and other circles, and to see the development that he had undergone in mind and character. I grew to respect him tremendously, and so had others apparently, for he was thoroughly qualified for the work that he did. My only sad thought was that we Americans had no diplomatic profession as such, that Bert served only at the "pleasure" (read whim) of the president. But this did not seem to concern him greatly; I believe he was now confident in his own ability.

I also enjoyed observing the Russians, whom I found very difficult to understand. There were undercurrents, I'm sure, of which I was completely unaware. I should not be surprised if a genuine revolution broke out soon. I found it very difficult to judge the character of the people, and I mentioned this in a letter to my brother Charles.

> The *gorodavoi*, or policemen are the nicest looking fellows I know in that capacity in any city, as far as possible from your big powerful London Bobby, and still further from the wild Irishmen of the New York street. They are rather small, active-looking young fellows, with faces beaming good humor, without any symbols of authority or force, standing all day long in the middle of the streets to reg ulate traffic and help people find the way, which they do most obligingly and even affectionately, with soft-toned manly voices But this does not prevent their being ready to obey the orders of their chiefs, were they to massacre all the inhabitants of Petersburg. The other day, a band of two or three hundred on horseback charged the body

of students of the university and beat many of them to jelly with heavy cavalry whips.

I did *not* tell Charles that I got to know one of those gorodavoi very well indeed. He was strikingly handsome, quite muscular, rather taller than the average. I was startled one day when he spoke to me in English; I had not expected the police to know my language. I found out later that he had been friendly with a former member of the American Legation, that they were in fact lovers. Sasha (the Russian—I never learned the American's name) was now thirty-five years old, an age that I usually find most attractive. After the American's departure he had continued to learn English and took every opportunity to improve. At first I thought this the only reason he wanted to speak to me. It soon became apparent that, with some quick intuition, he had realised that I was drawn to him, and he welcomed my interest. He was, as he said, "fond of older men." I needed no more encouragement; at my age I was determined to let no opportunity pass and I was soon seeing him regularly. He was, in fact, the reason I prolonged my stay in Russia.

Sasha had only one room, but he had furnished it so that it was very cosy. I wondered at first at the furniture, which seemed to me rather more expensive than I would have expected him to be able to afford. He told me that, on his departure, his American friend had left him a handsome sum of money. That was on my first visit to Sasha's room, and I told myself that, however nice Sasha might be, I would definitely not follow my country man's example. But that is just exactly what I did, for Sasha had a charm that could not be denied. One simply wanted to do things for him. You never had a feeling that he was trying to 'take' you. He did take my gifts, of course, and showed his gratitude. But I am convinced that he would have been just as friendly if I had given him nothing. It was always a pleasure to do things for him.

We spent little time together, for he worked very long hours, but sometimes I would shop for food—he gave me a list of items needed—and he would cook for the two of us on his tiny stove. I would also bring a bottle of fine wine (which he was not used to—it sometimes made him drowsy), so that our suppers were simple, but festive. Occasionally I bought caviar. That, too, he seldom had, but I think he did not appreciate it as much as I. To know caviar, one must come to the shores of the Baltic. It cannot be exported without salting and pressing, which greatly change it. Fresh, it is a dream.

After super, we would talk a bit and stroke one another's hands. Then one of us would say, "Shall we lie down?" We then lay together on his bed, usually he on his back and I beside and over him, my head on his breast, while he caressed my back. Or I would kiss him lightly on the lips and nestle my head in the angle of his neck and shoulder. Our time together was always short, for I had to leave and let him get his sleep for the next day. I tried desperately to store up the memory of how I felt then, to last me until the next time or for when . . .

I thought it best not to tell Bert about Sasha. (Sasha, of course, knew all about Bert.) So, when the time came, I said good-bye to them separately. Bert had not expected me to stay so long; I believe he was rather relieved when I left. Sasha simply took one day at a time, and did not feel the parting as such a sad event as I did. But he was the one who cried. I believe he was genuinely fond of me. For my part, I thought him one of the gems of the word; I left him as large a sum of money as I could conveniently spare.

In the end my departure was somewhat precipitous, for there were sudden threatenings of gallstone that I immediately recognised.

I hastily booked a trip on the railway for Karlsbad. I stayed at my former hotel, where I was an old friend, but vowed that on my next trip I would stay at the Grand Hotel Pupp, which was just then under construction and promised to be a magnificent structure. I imagined the grand view one would have from there, looking down over the town and the whole valley of the Tepl River!

The whole world eventually comes to Karlsbad, it seems, and one never knows whom he might meet. It was my good fortune on this visit to become acquainted with the noted mathematician Richard Dedekind, whose essay *Was sind und was sollen die Zahlen?* (What are and what should be numbers?) had appeared a decade earlier.[2] Peano had mentioned that booklet to me as anticipating some of his own discoveries; he had commented on how ideas seem at times to be "in the air" so that more than one person makes the same discovery almost simultaneously.

Richard Dedekind

Dedekind had retired from the Polytechnic in Brunswick three years earlier, at the age of sixty-five. He seemed to me to be in perfect health (he said the same of me), but had been advised by his doctor, because of certain difficulties, to drink the Sprudel water. As it happened, he was staying at my hotel, and when he learned that a Professor Peirce from America was there, he was curious to know which Peirce I was; he suspected Charles, whose work he was familiar with. I think he was disappointed at first, for he would have liked to discuss their common mathematical interests (he did not much care for quaternions); but in the end, I'm sure he was glad it was I he met, for we eventually

---

[2] Richard Dedekind (1831–1916), German mathematician, is known for his work on algebraic numbers and functions. His essay *Was sind und was sollen die Zahlen?* originated a theory of irrational numbers.

discussed a subject of some interest to him, which he had apparently discussed with no one before. I mean homosexuality.

Dedekind, as I soon suspected—and was eventually sure—was himself homosexual; but he had so hidden the fact, even from himself, that he could hardly face it even then. At an age when most men marry, he was already keeping house with his unmarried sister Julie, who was an accomplished writer. He was—or told himself that he was—content with his life. He had a comfortable home, he had his friends, he had his music circle, and above all, he had his mathematics. After his student days in Göttingen and a couple of years there as a Privatdozent, he had taught at the Polytechnic in Zurich for four years before returning to his hometown of Brunswick to become professor in the Polytechnic there. And there he remained for thirty-four years. He was offered more prestigious positions, but "modestly" chose to remain in Brunswick. From his stories of long hiking trips in the mountains with one of his colleagues, I think he must have been in love with him. But I doubt that much 'happened' between them.

[The following is from Peirce's notebook.]

Richard Dedekind

Dedekind is of average height, or a little shorter, thin and wiry, with closely trimmed gray hair and beard. He was diffident about his musical ability at first, but when he was finally persuaded to play for us on the piano in our hotel, he showed himself to be an accomplished musician. He very obviously loves music and even played a few compositions of his own. He gladly talks about his student days in Göttingen. I told him that I had met Wil helm Weber years before; he had many tales to tell of him. He also knew the great mathematician Gauß and was, so to speak, his last pupil. I have found him a warm-hearted and tolerant man. One day I found a way to bring the conversation around to the topic of homo sexuality. I was afraid at first that he would try to avoid the subject, but instead he listened in fascination.

"I have never discussed this with anyone," he told me. "For all practical purposes, I am 'married' to my sister, and everyone has accepted us as a couple. Perhaps Julie guessed that I am attracted to men, but we never mentioned it. For many years I struggled against my feelings, making no effort to understand them. When I finally began to accept myself, I was too old, too inexperienced, too fearful to seek partners. I clung to my home with Julie in little Brunswick; it meant safety to me. That is why I never accepted a position elsewhere."

"And mathematics is a safe subject," I added.

"Yes." He smiled, for I too had chosen mathematics. "And of course music furnishes an outlet for the emotions. Oh, I have had to be so discreet. I wonder sometimes what my life might have been, if I had been more daring." He sighed. "But I will not complain. It has been a comfortable life, and I have had affectionate friends."

"Do you disapprove of homosexual acts?" I asked bluntly.

"No," he said hesitantly, "not for others." He looked at me frankly. "But you appear so respectable and, well, manly. Have you really had many such experiences?"

"Many? Such things are relative. More than some people, and less than others. But yes, I have had sexual affairs with more than one man—though I have been truly in love with only one." I told him of Tom.

"That is wonderful," he remarked. "And do you really believe that he represents unspoiled man, your bisexual Tom?"

"I do indeed. I gather from your earlier comment about my 'manly' appearance that you know of other theories."

"I am not well read on the subject," he replied, "but I have heard that such men as ourselves, who are sexually attracted to other men, always have some feminine traits."

"All men have *some* feminine traits," I interrupted. "To point them out in the case of homosexuals and ignore them in the case of heterosexuals is simply to argue after the fact, an attempt to make the facts fit the theory."

"I see," he said. Obviously the thought was not new to him; I think he was pleased to find someone else who agreed with him. That conversation continued for some time, and was renewed the next day.

When I left Karlsbad the following morning, he shook my hand vigorously and thanked me for our discussion. "My dear Herr Peirce, I think you have done more for me on this visit than all the water from the Sprudel! Perhaps there is hope for the world after all—for people like us, I mean. You must try to spread your ideas. It won't be easy, of course, for most people are intolerant, but hopefully there will be a gradual improvement. I wish you luck!"

Dedekind occupied my thoughts for days afterward. I felt sorry for him, and did not know why. He had led a comfortable life, had a successful career and friends who must be fond of him. And yet, and yet . . . His real potential as a human being has not been realised, I finally thought. But who am I to judge? Nor was I as optimistic as he about the prospect for improvement in the situation of men like us. Perhaps the twentieth century will turn out all right, bye and bye, and a loving spirit will revive among men. But first we must emerge from this baleful *fin de siècle*, for the period in which we live at the present moment seems to me an odious one.

Little seemed to have changed in Cambridge during my absence. Everyone seemed to think the Mathematics Department to be there solely for the benefit of others. The University Crew, for example, were complaining that the advice on the shape and size of their oar blades, which Professor Hollis had given them a few years earlier, was wrong and that was why they lost their races. They demanded that we immediately direct our attention to finding out the very best shape and size, insisting that we give the project "urgent priority"!

Happily I was no longer Dean of the Faculty of Arts and Sciences, and so had more time for the Mathematics Department. And of course nothing prevented my continued enjoyment of the stage. The winter of 1899 is particularly memorable for the appearance in December of the incomparable Sir Henry Irving in Sardou's new play *Robespierre*.[3] A large party of us went in two hacks to the theatre and were afterwards joined for supper by Irving and his manager Bram Stoker, whose mystery thriller *Dracula* was such a success two years earlier.[4] We toasted him for that, and of course toasted Irving on his evening's performance as well as his knighthood. We saw it as a personal tribute that he was the first English actor to be so honored. He modestly replied that he saw it rather as a recognition of the advance of his profession. I was amused to see how all the democratic Americans seemed eager to address him as "Sir Henry."

I had enjoyed seeing Irving and his leading lady Ellen Terry[5] several times in Shakespearean productions at the Lyceum Theatre in London, and I recall him with special pleasure in Conan Doyle's *The Story of Waterloo* during my brief stop in London in 1894. He "reigned supreme on the English stage," as more than one critic wrote.

Bram Stoker modestly chose to sit at the foot of the table opposite Irving. I sat on his right and, the number being too large for general conversation, had a most delightful private chat with him. I opened it by remarking that first novels were usually autobiographical, and

[3] Henry Irving (1838–1905), English actor. Born John Henry Brodribb, he later legally assumed his stage name Henry Irving.

[4] Bram Stoker (1847–1912), British writer. In addition to several novels, Stoker also wrote his *Personal Reminiscences of Henry Irving*. Noting Stoker's early letters to Walt Whitman and his long relationship with Irving, Jonathan Ned Katz suggested, "Stoker's own sexual orientation merits investigation," in his *Gay American History: Lesbians and Gay Men in the U.S.A.* (New York: Thomas Y. Crowell, 1965), p. 605. For the relationship between Stoker and Irving, see also John D'Addario, "Bram Stoker and the Homoeroticism of Vampires," *The Advocate*, October 24, 1989, pp. 40–42.

[5] Ellen Alicia Terry (1848–1928), English actress, had a long and successful career. She first appeared on the stage at the age of eight and celebrated her stage-jubilee in 1906.

I facetiously asked, "Is *Dracula* your first novel?" It was not, as I knew, but he laughed, and the ice was broken. I found him a charming supper companion, certainly far from the sinister Count Dracula of his tale. He did indicate, however, that certain traits in the novel were drawn from some "blood suckers" connected with the theatre. Most interesting was his discussion of how his knowledge of the stage, gained from his association with Irving, had helped him to construct certain scenes. He would visualise them being acted on the stage and then write a description of what he saw. He also claimed that the awful suspense that builds up for the reader of *Dracula* was partly a result of his theatrical observations. I was fascinated, gaining new insights into writers, actors, and—vampires.

The year 1900 began and ended with requests for money from Charles. He seemed determined to die. I wonder that I did not simply send him a telegram: "So die already!" But I did not—coward that I am. In December 1900, for example, he complained terribly of being cold and hungry, but when I visited him and Juliette only a week after that letter, I found them very comfortable on the whole. Arisbe, their home in Milford, Pennsylvania, was delightful.

The big event in my own home in 1901 was the marriage of my niece Sally[6] to Richard Colbis. The reception was in my home. We all said we wanted as little fuss as possible, but in fact there was much to do and think about—and it turned out to be rather expensive. Still, it was nice, and I was glad I could do it for her. I thought I could relax afterward, but the heat in July was tremendous, at least I felt it more than usual, and I looked forward to a cool ocean voyage—though, as usual, I dreaded becoming seasick.

---

[6] Sarah Ellis, daughter of Peirce's sister Helen.

FOURTEEN
LONG LIVE QUATERNIONS!

I SAILED FOR Europe by the Grosser Kurfürst on July 25, 1901, for two months in Eu rope, going first to Bayreuth for the Wagner Musikfest. It was, as always, a great joy for me. I could accept the fact that Clifford did not appreciate the music of Wagner, but I wondered how it was that Dedekind, a musician himself, did not like it. I had vaguely planned to join Professor Bôcher in France, but decided that I really wanted simply to rest. I also wanted to remain in the German-speaking region, where I felt more comfortable than in France. A chance acquaintance in Bayreuth suggested just the place for me: Pettau, south of Vienna, in the province of Styria.[1]

[The following is from Peirce's diary.]

Pettau is an ancient town on the Drau river; it was the Roman Poetavio. The current population is about 4,000. It is a linguistic island, in that the town itself is German speaking, whereas the surrounding countryside speaks a Slavic language. Living is very cheap; I am seriously

---
[1] Pettau, now Ptuj, has been Slovenian since 1919.

considering moving over here when I go on the retired list. The weather is cooler than I had expected, so that I have greatly enjoyed my walks along the river. The Slavic influence is easily seen in the appearance of the people. I notice most particularly the lack of body hair on the men and boys, many of whom are strikingly handsome. All treat me with respect; perhaps they are influenced by my long beard. Does it give me the look of a sage?

Tuesday, August 27, 1901. Yesterday I had a charming conversation with two lads, aged perhaps 16 and 17. They overtook me as I was walking beside the river and asked for the time. I think they only wanted to start a conversation, to see who I was. They were going into the river at a point further up stream, they said. They were, however, already wet, so I asked if they had not already been swimming.

"Oh yes, but the river current is too fast to swim against it. So we just let it take us a ways, then get out and walk back."

When we reached the spot where they were to go into the water, I stopped to watch them. They must have seen my admiration, for instead of going directly into the water they sat beside me on the river bank and continued our lively discussion. I thought they might be brothers, but no, it turned out that they were fellow apprentices in a bakery. They were off for the rest of the afternoon since their work began very early in the morning. They were curious about me and my travels, for they had never been away from Pettau and envied me greatly. I, on the other hand, envied them their beauty and natural grace, and their apparent ease with one another. It was clear right away that they were fond of each another as they held hands and stroked one another in a completely natural, unembarrassed way.

After talking a while I sat in the shade, while they had stretched out in the sun, lying side by side. At one point the older lad laid his arm over the other, who playfully shoved it away. A mild wrestling match ensued, whose object, whether this was conscious or not, was obviously the enjoyment of body contact, for I soon noticed that the bulge in each crotch was becoming large. Then one put his hand over the bulge of the other and began to gently massage. The other relaxed onto his back, and then stiffened to look over at me. I pretended to be intently examining the back of my hand, and he again relaxed. The first lad too had glanced in my direction, but apparently satisfied that I was unconcerned, he had returned his attention to his friend. Then he leaned over and tenderly kissed him on the mouth. The response was a warm, tight embrace.   Thus they lay on their sides, their nearly naked bodies pressed closely together, and I noticed a slight grinding motion of their hips, which gradually became more intense. The younger of the two came first. I saw a slight convulsion, heard a small sound, and then he relaxed while the older, now on top of his friend, continued his motions. Soon he too must have reached a climax, for he quivered, threw his head back, and then slumped onto the receptive body beneath him.

I was so absorbed in observing all this that I did not notice my own arousal until I felt a moistness against my leg. I glanced down to see a spot on my trousers. When I looked up again, the two boys had fallen apart and were now lying side by side on their backs. They too showed wet spots in their clothing, which was entirely wet when I first saw them, but had quickly dried in the sun The fingers of their hands were entwined. It was a wonderful and touching scene. They were so beautiful! I wanted to hug them both to me at once, to run my hands over their smooth, perfect skin, to kiss those lips and nipples, and, yes, bury my face in their groins and breathe in the luscious odor of sex from their youthful bodies.

I breathed in deeply, and sighed. How achingly beautiful youth is! And I recalled the lines of Lorenzo the Magnificent:

> *Quant'è bella giovinezza,*
> *Che si fugge tuttavia.*

Yes, youth is beautiful—but fleeting. I stood up quietly and left the boys still lying in the sun with eyes closed and a smile of contentment on each face. The wet spots had nearly dried.

I wonder what has become of the two lads I met in Pettau. They are of an age to marry now. Have they taken wives, or do they still have one another? Or—and I think this most likely—has one married and the other had to resign himself to a second place, perhaps a very distant second, in the affections of his friend? I have decided against moving there when I retire, but perhaps I shall return to visit one day. Would I recognise them again?

My return trip across the Atlantic was not as pleasant as the trip over. We ran into a couple of storms, my old seasickness returned, and on top of that I caught a bad cold that stayed with me for weeks. But I was determined to make my mark on mathematics, so as soon as I was settled I set to work in earnest on the treatise on quaternions that I had projected for some time. I wanted to finish, before I die, something that would be a real contribution to quaternions and promote their continued and more advanced study. But a treatise is a big job, and though I had a good many materials, the actual licking into shape was sure to lead to much writing and rewriting. I had the introductory chapter ready by October, but thought I had better send it to Charles for his comments before spending more time on the project. So I sent a typewritten copy to him that month—along with my usual cheque. "I might as well get some return for my money," I thought. It was a mistake; his criticisms were so severe that I set the project aside in depression, and in the end I lost all enthusiasm for it.

The year ended near tragically. My servant Thomas was thrown off a trolley street car on Christmas day and broke his hip bone. I had to take care of him, and I think it was only the reversal in our roles that kept him cheerful. A year later he was still on crutches; he never felt well enough to return to my service.

My own mortality was impressed on me shortly after Thomas's accident. In January 1902 I caught another of my bad colds and had a strange dread that it would pass into a regular bronchitis. And just about then two of my acquaintances dropped dead quite unexpectedly. My cold lingered into the spring, but I gradually regained my composure.

In April I was asked to expand my biographical sketch of Father for *Lamb's Biograph ical Dictionary*. I hated to approach Charles again, but I knew he would expect to be consulted, so with some trepidation I sent him my article. This time, to my relief, he entirely approved. In fact, he thought it "quite admirable."

That summer I again returned to Karlsbad. I sailed for Bremen in July and proceeded directly there, for I felt that my health was not what it should be. This time I stayed at the new Grand Hotel Pupp. I was amused by the name of the hotel (for "Pupp" in German means "fart," if I am not mistaken) and wished I had John Henry Mackay's address; I wanted to write to him that I could now call myself a "Puppenjunge." He had told me that the boy prostitutes in Berlin were called that.[2] I was tempted to go to Berlin and see for myself, but in the end decided I had better stay a bit longer at Karlsbad with my fellow sufferers. (Not that there were many real sufferers in the Grand Hotel Pupp; most of the guests were obviously there for the social and political contacts.) I was convinced that the waters did me good, but later in November I had another sharp attack, followed in a few weeks by yet another.

Charles had gained some recognition for his articles on pragmatism. Thus when William James asked my advice about inviting him to Harvard to lecture on the subject, I heartily supported the suggestion. Besides, it would certainly help his financial situation. Charles was pleased with the invitation and in fact gave a series of eight lectures beginning in late March 1903. In early March I was in Baltimore representing the University at the dinner of the Harvard

---

[2] In 1926 Mackay published a novel with the title *Der Puppenjunge*, which deals with the lives of boy prostitutes in Berlin. The usual spelling of the word, however, is Pupenjunge (i.e., without the double-p), and it is so spelled throughout the text of the novel. *Der Puppenjunge* appeared in English translation as *The Hustler* (Boston: Alyson, 1985). Peirce was half-right: The German word "Pup" (without the double-p) means "fart" (pupen = to fart).

Club there. I proceeded on to Washington to visit my brother Bert, who had returned there from St. Petersburg to assume the duties of his new appointment as third assistant secretary of state. We agreed to lend Charles the money to pay his current mortgage expenses: Bert $100, and I $50.

James invited Charles to stay at his house during the period of his Harvard lectures, but I thought it better if he stayed with me, even though my house was already a bit crowded. (My brother-in-law, Will Ellis, had died at the beginning of February, and Helen and her children were already living with me.) It was a trying time for all of us; the servant "department" became very disgruntled. But Charles made a good impression with his lectures, and there was already talk of his returning at the end of the year to lecture at the Lowell Institute. He was well paid for his lectures, but insisted that it hardly covered his debts. Thus he was again badgering me for money. I sent some to Juliette, but wrote Charles in June:

> I am very sorry that when I do the best I am able to afford, it seems to you insufficient.
>
> I am trying to do what I can for you. It is little enough relatively to your needs, I admit. But it involves some effort for me, and it must go as far as it will.

I fear that sounded rather unfeeling; it was not meant so. But I could not just then see my way to helping him in the way he wanted.

In June my old enemy, the gallstone, attacked again, no doubt brought on by the celebration of my class Jubilee. The observance of the 50th anniversary of our graduation began with a Clark's Union Club dinner, which was followed the next day by a luncheon in University

Hall and then a tea at my house. The tea cost me much worry; it seemed as if everything was going wrong. But finally I did have all in readiness, and the event was generally pronounced "delightful." The result for me, however, was that I was a wreck. Tom jokingly said that I would have to drink up all the waters of Karlsbad before being able to digest a boiled egg. He was very nearly right.

My trip across the Atlantic, despite all my dread of seasickness, proved to be quite pleasant, and I felt well enough to stop a week in Munich before going on to Karlsbad. The "Richard Wagner Festival Plays" began at the Prinz-Regenten Theater the second week in August. In addition to the *Ring of the Nibelung*, four other operas were presented. I saw as many of them as I could in a week; Karlsbad then became a necessity for me, if only for the rest it offered.

In the fall it was arranged for Charles to give eight lectures at the Lowell Institute in November and December. That would bring him some money, of course, but in October he insisted that I give him something immediately for repairs to his house. I recalled my earlier experience and was reluctant to send any money without first seeing for myself how necessary the repairs were. Besides I was pretty hard up myself, for I was almost the sole support of a rather large household. I advised Charles to take another mortgage and pay back the $150 he owed Bert and me. I also declined to have him stay at my house while in Cambridge; I felt unable to take upon myself any added responsibility or expense, or add to the work of my servants.

Charles's lectures were well received, and the money did indeed help him pay off some old debts, but I think he never got 'ahead' for he seemed to have always new, unexpected expenses. He inquired about my treatise on quaternions. I told him I had abandoned it; I did not tell him the precise reason. He urged me to do something with the subject, not to let my expertise die with me. I then renewed my determination to put into an article the original thoughts I had on the subject, but leave treatise writing to others.

Through the winter and the spring of 1904 I worked on my article, whose object was to extend the application of quaternions to the field of projective geometry, which had hitherto been closed to quaternions. This was done by the introduction of the duality principle and the principle of homogeneous coordinates. I completed my paper in April and presented it at the end of that month to the American Mathematical Society; it was later published in their *Transactions*.[3]

This time my paper was well received; but there seemed to be a general opinion that the popularity of the theory had passed and that even such efforts as mine could not awaken to new life the calculus of quaternions. Still, I was pleased that I had finally made what I knew to be a genuinely original, if late contribution. My article on quaternions in *Johnson's New Universal Cyclopedia* a quarter century earlier had been much praised. Its only originality had been in the manner of presentation. Had I published this new article at that time I have no doubt it would have made a grand splash in the mathematical world. But I will not complain. The day after I presented that paper to the Society, I celebrated my seventieth birthday. I was pleased with what I had done, and I think some of the members were astonished, for original mathematics is generally thought to be the province of the younger mathematicians.

I am not young and cannot live much longer. But I shall die content with my life. I regret the missed opportunities, the wrong turns in my youth, the indecision in my choice of career—but all that would have been hard to avoid. Above all, I feel that I have been deprived

---

[3] "On Certain Complete Systems of Quaternion Expressions, and on the Removal of Metric Limitations from the Calculus of Quaternions." See appendix B.

of the love and sexual fulfillment that should have been there, but was prevented by the madness of the society in which we live. Even the much vaunted Enlightenment had hardly been 'enlightened' in matters sexual, and I feel we have made little advancement since. Will the time ever come, I wonder, when the love of a man for a man, the love of a woman for a woman, be accepted on a par with the love of a man and a woman for each other? Ulrichs thought he had found a new, profound truth—and like most prophets thought he had only to announce it for the world to receive it with open arms. Instead, his 'truth' was received with disgust, rejection, and mean-spirited pettiness.

Ulrichs's ideas have been taken up again, with some modification, by Dr. Hirschfeld and his associates in Berlin.[4] They seem to be having some success, and yet I think they cannot eventually succeed in their quest, for Ulrichs's theory is ultimately unsound. Mackay is more realistic there; but even if he ever begins to make propaganda for his cause, he works in such "splendid isolation"—to use one of his frequent English phrases—that he can have little effect.[5]

I had hoped for a while that Symonds would come out of his timorous attitude of treading ever so carefully and gently in the field, but his death came much too early, and Ellis is obviously not prepared to follow even that lead. Indeed, I believe Ellis saw it as a distraction from his own goals—whatever they are. But was I any more daring than any of them? Certainly not; not even more daring than Symonds, not to mention the incomparable Ulrichs.

In the end, we must each make our own life. But the influence of

---

[4] The Scientific Humanitarian Committee (Berlin), founded in 1897, had as its primary mission the revision of the German law against homosexual acts. Its goal was not attained, and the Committee dissolved when the Nazis came to power in 1933.

[5] In fact, Mackay did begin a struggle in 1905 to gain wider acceptance for man-boy love, but his efforts were crushed by the state. This is detailed in "The History of a Fight for the Nameless Love," in *Sagitta's Books of the Nameless Love* (pp. 13–48), edited and translated by Hubert Kennedy (Concord, CA: Peremptory Publications, 2005).

others cannot be denied. Had I never met Tom, what would my life be like? The question is unanswerable, and yet I am very aware of how important he has been to me. There were years when I never saw him, years when I saw him but seldom, and yet he made a difference. His acceptance of me, his support, his genuine affection gave me a security I might never have otherwise felt. My love for him was passionate aching; it mellowed to a warm friendship that has endured and endures. In August 1904 I stayed a few days with him and Lilla in their home in Hancock, New Hampshire. Tom asked me to sign their Guest Book. "Lilla insists that it be kept properly," he said, almost in embarrassment, "but I cannot think of you as a 'guest.' You belong here, old friend." Tears welled up in my eyes. He wrapped his arms around me, and for a moment the memories of years long past swept over me. I think I never felt more alive.

In the summer of 1905 I again went to Europe, but unlike earlier trips I spent most of my time in England. When he was very young Charles once said that life was of little value unless you made some advance in the family genealogy; he meant, of course, to have children. As it turned out, neither he nor I did that. But now, for some reason, I became interested in tracing our genealogy backwards. I knew that my great-great-great-great-great-grandfather John Pers, a weaver, emigrated to New England from Norwich in April 1637. I went there to try to learn more about him if possible. Alas, I could find nothing about him personally, but I did get an indication of his origin. It seems altogether probable that he was of Flemish extraction and I guess that his father or grandfather may have come over. In 1894 I had found the name Peers in the Directory of Ghent. It was of course pronounced with the same vowel sound that we now have in "heir" and was naturally Englished as Peirce, though John's name is always written

Pers. John's son Robert, from whom I issue, spelled his name Peirce, and all the generations of Robert's descendants have so spelled it.

I found the area around Norwich lovely and relaxing, but it was the excitement of the London theatres that I continued to enjoy. I thought that, as I grew older, I would no longer feel the spell of the theatre so strongly, but that has not been the case. Even when I was on my way from England to take my steamer at Genoa and had two nights in Paris, I spent both of those nights at the Théâtre Français. Here in Boston there is also much to enjoy. I write "here," for it is now so easy to go into Boston from Cambridge that I hardly think of myself as living in another town. That was not so when I was young! Then it was a real excursion to brave the cold and poor roads. Of course, when I was young I was better able to endure those difficulties and, as young people will, saw only the adventure in it.

And now I have brought my memoirs up to date. I wonder when I shall take them up again. Perhaps never. I am seventy-one years old. How much longer can I live?

I can only hope and trust that, one day, when these memoirs will have been published, they will furnish a motive of encouragement for readers to take charge of their lives, to reject the useless 'authority' that tries to tell them how to live, that pretends to know 'what is best' for them. And you, dear reader, receive my greetings and warmest wishes for a life of love and, yes, sexual fulfillment!

James Mills Peirce
Cambridge, November 27, 1905

[This is the last record in his memoirs. James Mills Peirce died of pneumonia on 21 March 1906 after a brief illness.]

APPENDIX A
OBITUARIES

The following appeared in the *Boston Herald* of 22 March 1906:

Prof. Peirce, Harvard, Dead

Professor James Mills Peirce, A.M., Perkins professor of astronomy and mathematics, died at his home, 4 Kirkland Place, Cambridge, yesterday afternoon, after an illness of less than one week. He met his classes a week ago, and after returning home was found to be suffering from an attack of bronchitis which was not serious enough to cause alarm. Tuesday he felt apparently well, but late in the afternoon pneumonia set in, and the congestion was so rapid that he died in less than twenty-four hours after being attacked.

Last week his resignation from the Harvard faculty was accepted, to take effect March 1, 1907, on which date he would have finished fifty years as a teacher at Harvard. His death removes one of the oldest members of the Harvard faculty, a man who was prominent in the development of the Lawrence Scientific School and in the inception of the graduate school, of which for five years he was dean, resigning 1895, after which he was dean of the faculty of arts and sciences for three years. He was a widely known mathematician, being considered the world's authority on quaternions, and the author of many textbooks of mathematics, among which are "Textbook of Analytic Geometry," "Three and Four Place Tables," "Elements of Logarithms," and "Mathematical Tables Chiefly to Four Figures," and has contributed many valuable papers on astronomy and mathematics.

His father was Professor Benjamin Peirce, who for many years was professor of astronomy and mathematics at Harvard, and who died in 1882. One brother is Hon. Herbert H. D. Peirce, recently appointed the first United States minister to Norway, formerly third assistant Secretary of State. Another brother is Charles Sanders Peirce, who is one of the greatest living authorities on logic, psychology and philosophy, lecturer at Harvard and living in Milford, Pa. His only sister is Mrs. W. R. Ellis of Cambridge, with whom he lived.

Professor Peirce was born in Cambridge May 1, 1834. He received the degree of A.M. from Harvard with the class of 1853, having among his classmates President Eliot and Professor S. Hill. He tutored in Cambridge until 1858 and three years later was made assistant professor in mathematics. From 1869 until 1885 he was university professor of the same subject and was then appointed to the position of Perkins professor of astronomy and mathematics. He was secretary of the academic council from 1872 until 1890, and for the next five years was dean of the graduate school.

He was a member of the St. Botolph Club and the Shelley Society of Boston and the Players' Club, University Club and Harvard Club of New York, where he was prominently known. He never married.

Professor Peirce, though known as a student of higher mathematics to the world in general, was a patron of the arts, being a great lover of poetry and the theatre. He was an omnivorous reader of the poetry and literature of all races.

The following contain personal recollections:

Byerly, W. E. "James Mills Peirce." *Harvard Graduates' Magazine* 14 (1906): 573–477.

Rantoul, R. S. "James Mills Peirce." *Report of the Harvard Class of 1853, 1849–1913* (1913): 208–213.

Whittemore, J. K. "James Mills Peirce." *Science* 24 (1906), No. 602: 40–48.

At the request of the editor of the *Harvard Graduates' Magazine*, T. S. Perry sent a sketch of Peirce, which was printed as a footnote to the article by W. E. Byerly. Because of Perry's intimate knowledge of Peirce, the concluding paragraph is of particular interest:

> He had many friends old and young. His old friends he kept, and to do that is an art; he made new ones and young ones. He had a great fondness for the young who are really young, as he was himself till the day of his death. He was a fiery soul and he understood and sympathized with their enthusiasm, and hopes and eagerness, because he too was enthusiastic, hopeful and eager. His fervour, his intensity made him a marked figure in a world where there are more counters than coins. He sympathized intensely with good and honourable things and hated what was odious with equal intensity. He was no friend of compromise. A vivid figure is gone from Cambridge.

APPENDIX B

Annotated List of Publications by James Mills Peirce

The Character and Philosophy of Malebranche. *Monthly Religious Magazine* 15 (1858): 373–399. This article is an excellent analysis of the philosophy of Malebranche, seen as a development of that of Descartes.

A Text-Book of Analytic Geometry; on the Basis of Professor Peirce's Treatise. Cambridge, MA: Bartlett, 1857. vii + 228 pp., 6 plates. This is based on his father's text, but the treatment is much more detailed.

Charles Russell Lowell. *Harvard Memorial Biographies*, 2 vols. Cambridge, MA: Sever & Francis, 1866. 1: 296–327. Peirce was a friend of the Lowell family whose son, Charles Russell Lowell, Jr., died in the Civil War.

Three and Four Place Tables of Logarithmic and Trigonometric Functions. Boston, 1869. 16 pp.

The Elements of Logarithms, with an Explanation of the Three and Four Place Tables of Logarithmic and Trigonometric Functions. Boston, 1873. vi + 83 pp. This publication adds instructions to the tables above, with examples showing how to use them.

Quaternions. *Johnson's New Universal Cyclopedia*. New York: A. J. Johnson & Son, 1877. 3: 1491–1493. This is an excellent short introduction to the theory of quaternions.

References in Analytic Geometry. *Harvard College Library Bulletin* 1 (1878): 157–158, 246–250, 289–290. This is a brief summary of the work of François Viète, followed by a masterly analysis of Descartes's *Géométrie*. Priority questions are also discussed and Peirce is careful to point out the motivations Descartes found in the work of Viète and others. Peirce here shows himself to be a very able historian of mathematics.

Mathematical Tables, Chiefly to Four Figures. First Series. Boston: Ginn & Heath, 1879. This useful set of tables was reprinted at least ten times during Peirce's lifetime.

Rule Relating to the Calendar. *The Harvard Register* 3 (1881): 361. Peirce accurately describes his calendar in the opening sentence: "The following rule for ascertaining the day of the week on which any date of the Christian era falls is easily carried in the memory, and may often be found useful." The calculations required are not difficult and the method is indeed memorable.

Ideality in the Physical Sciences, by Benjamin Peirce, edited by J. M. Peirce. Boston: Little, Brown & Co., 1881. vi + 211 pp. Plans for publication of six lectures delivered by Benjamin Peirce in 1879 at the Lowell Institute in Boston were interrupted by his death on 6 October 1880. J. M. Peirce's contributions to this volume were a preface describing the origin of the lectures, footnotes citing sources he believed his father had used, and an appendix (pp. 197–211) in which he gives the views of his father on some matters not completely worked out in the lectures, principally concerning a rather dubious conjecture about the discovery of the planet Neptune.

An Outline of Plane Analytic Geometry for the Use of Students in Mathematics C, 1887–88. Cambridge, MA, 1888. 68 pp. Despite the modest title, this is a thorough summary of plane analytic geometry through the theory of curves of the second degree.

Remarks at the Dinner of the Harvard Club of New York, 20 February 1891. Cambridge, MA. 11 pp. Peirce here shows himself to be an accomplished after-dinner speaker, in an able defense of graduate study.

Theoretical knowledge and practical facility in algebra: To what extent is each important in preparation for college? *School and College* 1 (1892): 535–540.

The Graduate School. *Annual Reports, 1894–95.* Cambridge, MA: Harvard University, 1895, pp. 101–133. This was Peirce's last report as Dean of the Graduate School. Besides the usual statistical information, this report is of interest for Peirce's rationale behind the newly established John Harvard Fellowships and his valedictory comments on his office.

Zusatz zu Kapital II. In *Das konträre Geschlechtsgefühl,* by Havelock Ellis and J. A. Symonds, trans. Hans Kurella, Leipzig: Georg H. Wigand's Verlag, 1896, pp. 277–279. This is a translation of the following publication, but appeared earlier because of the difficulty in finding a publisher in England.

Letter from Professor X. In *Sexual Inversion,* by Havelock Ellis and J. A. Symonds. London: Wilson & Macmillan, 1897, pp. 273–275. This letter is an extraordinarily strong defense of homosexuality.

Determinants of Quaternions. *Bulletin of the American Mathematical Society* (2) 5 (1899): 335–337. Peirce here extended the theory of determinants to include quaternions. He saw his principal result as the connection between linear equations of quaternions and determinants of quaternions.

Benjamin Peirce. *Lamb's Biographical Dictionary of the United States*. John Howard Brown, ed. Boston, 1903. 6: 196–198.

On Certain Complete Systems of Quaternion Expressions, and on the Removal of Metric Limitations from the Calculus of Quaternions. *Transactions of the American Mathematical Society* 5 (1904): 411–420. This article is original, creative, and directly within the quaternion tradition. Peirce stated as its object: "I shall show that it is easy to introduce into quaternions the principle of the *dualism of points and planes* familiar in modern analysis, and the principle of *homogeneousness*, which gives so great an advantage in projective geometry to tetrahedral over Cartesian coordinates, also to assume arbitrarily *any four linearly independent quaternions* as the fundamental geometric elements, and thus entirely to discard from our system all metric ideas."

APPENDIX C
THE THEORY OF
QUATERNIONS

IN THE SECOND half of the nineteenth century the mathematical theory of quaternions enjoyed an enormous vogue on both sides of the Atlantic, so much so that there was formed an International Association for Promoting the Study of Quaternions and Allied Systems of Mathematics. By early in the twentieth century, however, the theory was out of favor, and the organization was laughingly called "The Society for the Prevention of Cruelty to Quaternions." Since the theory of quaternions will thus be unfamiliar to most readers, even those with a mathematical background, the following brief introduction may be of interest. This was the theory to which J. M. Peirce devoted most of his mathematical energy.

The system of quaternions, based on four units (the real number 1 and three 'imaginaries' i, j, k) was discovered—or invented—by the Irish mathematician William Rowan Hamilton in 1843, after searching for many years in vain for a 'number' system based on three units. Hamilton had hoped to find a system that could be represented in three-dimensional space in a way analogous to the representation of complex numbers in the plane. Complex numbers (numbers of the form $a + bi$, where a and b are real numbers and i is the 'imaginary' unit such that $i^2 = -1$) arose in the solution of algebraic equations, but it was the possibility of representing them as points in a plane, where the complex number $3 + 4i$, for example, is graphed as the point with rectangular coordinates (3,4), that gave them their ultimate respectability in the early nineteenth century. Hamilton sought a similar system of three units, to be represented in three-dimensional space, but was unable to find a consistent multiplication rule. We now know that such a system is impossible. But one day in 1843, while out walking with his wife, the multiplication rule came to him for a 'number' system based on four units: the real number 1 and the three imaginaries i, j, k.

A quaternion (the name comes from the Latin word *quattuor*, or four) is an expression of the form $a + bi + cj + dk$, where a, b, c, d are real numbers and the imaginaries i, j, k are such that $i^2 = j^2 = k^2 = ijk = -1$. Quaternions may be added and multiplied with the usual rules of arithmetic, and the   result written in the required form by replacing i^2 with -1, ij with k, etc. Thus quaternions are a generalization of real and complex numbers in the sense that each of these systems is contained in the arithmetic of quaternions. Quaternions may be added and multiplied, just as in those two systems—with one exception to the rules: multiplication is not commutative, that is, the product of two quaternions is usually not the same as their product in reverse order.

That quaternion multiplication is not commutative seemed to Hamilton a small sacrifice to make for a general system that was otherwise entirely consistent with the other number systems. It did not seem small to many of his contemporaries, who saw it as contradicting the concept of number—and they cast doubt on its very existence. The theory was not *discovered*, they said, but was *invented* by Hamilton. Nor could quaternions be represented by points in space as complex

HUBERT KENNEDY

numbers were represented by points in the plane. Hamilton had no difficulty in representing the 'imaginary' part $bi + cj + dk$ by the point with rectangular coordinates (b,c,d), but what about the real part? His suggestion that this represented time was hardly convincing.

Thus, quaternions might have remained an almost unnoticed mathematical curiosity, if it had not been possible to apply them to the study of the physical world. Hamilton set himself the task of showing that this could be done, and he succeeded brilliantly. He soon had an enthusiastic following on both sides of the Atlantic. Only five years after their discovery, the theory of quaternions was the subject of a course given at Harvard University by Benjamin Peirce (1808–1880). Peirce remained a champion of quaternions the rest of his life, and his son James Mills Peirce (1834–1906), who followed in his father's footsteps as professor of mathematics at Harvard University, also continued this tradition of interest in quaternions. From 1878 J. M. Peirce regularly offered a two-year course in the subject, and he published original research on quaternions as late as 1904, only two years before his death. By then, however, the theory of quaternions had lost much of its popularity, for Hamilton's very success carried with it the seeds of its own destruction. One of Hamilton's most important uses for quaternions was in the application of certain quaternion expressions—he called them "vectors"—to the study of physical motion. Physicists, such as J. W. Gibbs of Yale University, saw that if only parts of quaternion theory were used, especially vectors, then the calculations could be greatly simplified and the physical applications made more immediate. In the early 1880s he published his system of "vector analysis." Although Gibb's theory lacked the elegance so prized by mathematicians, it proved more useful in practice, so that by 1900 its use by physicists had nearly replaced the use of quaternions in their research.

The theory of quaternions was not proved false, it simply ceased to be of much interest. To be sure, there has been a small, but continued use of quaternions in the study of theoretical physics. Students of mathematics mostly come across the theory in their study of modern abstract algebra, as an example of the structure known as a noncommutative division ring. They find it difficult to understand why there was opposition to quaternions as an algebraic system. But from a historical viewpoint, we may appreciate the breakthrough that the theory of quaternions represented. It was 'self-evident' to most of Hamilton's contemporaries that multiplication *must* be commutative. By furnishing a system whose practical advantages outweighed the loss of commutativity in multiplication he opened the path to a broader understanding of what constitutes an 'algebraic' system and to the great variety of structures in modern abstract algebra. With the development of vector analysis, much of the utility of quaternion theory was lost. But by then our view of mathematics had changed. The distinction between discovery and invention in mathematics had lost much of its force, and the way to newer algebraic structures had been opened.

From: Hubert Kennedy, "Who Needs Quaternions?" *New England Mathematics Journal* 29.1 (1986): 14–16.

HUBERT KENNEDY
FACT AND FICTION

IN HIS WONDERFUL *The Reader's Encyclopedia* (1948) William Rose Benét gave the following definition:

> *Professorenroman.* (*Ger.*). Literally, "professor's novel."
> In German literary history a very convenient term applied to novels which are crammed full of reliably correct historical detail but which remain absolutely devoid of literary inspiration.

Despite Benét's harsh conclusion, I like to see my little Professorenroman as being in the tradition of such novels, which indeed had a great vogue in the second half of the nineteenth century in Germany. They often treated contemporary problems set in the past and many were extremely successful. The most outstanding example is Felix Dahn's *Ein Kampf um Rom* (1876; in English as *A Struggle for Rome*, 1878), which has been in print since its first publication.

More recently Umberto Eco's *The Name of the Rose* has been described as a Professorenroman. That is good company indeed!

As the reviewer of a book by another mathematics professor wrote: "What was earlier disparagingly referred to as a Professorenroman can, in this era of edutainment, definitely be an adventure."

When I published the first edition of *Sex and Math in Harvard Yard*, I sent copies to several acquaintances I thought would be interested. One distinguished historian of mathematics immediately wrote back demanding to know the location of James Mills Peirce's sex diary. Alas, I had to reply that he had overlooked the phrase "fictional biography" on the title page and that the sex diary was my invention. I was secretly pleased that he thought it could be real, for that, of course, was my intention.

Readers who accept the milieu descriptions in the book as accurate may still legitimately wonder how much of my picture of Peirce is factual, apart from such obviously fictional elements as conversations, etc.

First, I suppose it is clear that all footnotes are meant to be accurate. The places where the description is based on actual observation or on published material are too numerous to mention. As examples: A music critic did describe Emma Eames's Aida as "skating on the Nile" and her introduction to trills was pointed out to me by the owner of a wonderful collection of old recordings when he played for me one of her singing. Peirce probably did use the recently invented "letter-press" method of copying typewritten letters. Harvard football players were indeed called "chrysanthemum heads".

Much more important for the biography of Peirce are the letters I quote from. All are real, with one exception: part of the "Professor X" letter to John Addington Symonds. It is clear that the letter as published by Havelock Ellis lacks a beginning and an end. I added a couple of short paragraphs at the beginning and at the end to make the letter appear complete.

I spent all of a Christmas college holiday commuting daily from Providence to Boston on the New York, New Haven and Hartford Railroad, to take the subway to Harvard Yard in order to read Peirce letters in the Houghton Library. It was on my very last day there that I found the letter from Peirce to Thomas Sergeant Perry. It gave me the proof I needed of the attachment of Peirce to Perry and gave me the central point of the story. That made the search worth all the train rides in the cold and the dark, for the old New Haven cars were often without heat or lights.

Peirce wrote in a letter that he intended to visit Symonds in Davos Platz, but I have no evidence that he actually did. I, however, went to Davos Platz and viewed Symonds's house there, and so could describe it. Peirce did visit his brother in St. Petersburg and also took the waters at Karlsbad. That he met the mathematician Richard Dedekind there, and the mathematician Giuseppe Peano in Turin, is my imagination, as are the meetings in Italy with Ulrichs and Mackay, two pioneers of the homosexual emancipation movement in Germany. Nevertheless I think there is nothing in those meetings that is out of character for those personalities. I have made a special study, and have written biographies, of the last three.

There is a saying that all first novels are autobiographical. *Sex and Math in Harvard Yard* is my first (and only) novel and I won't deny that the saying applies here too. It is probably best that I not go into this. But I can't pass up mentioning one instance, namely the charming young man in Freiburg, with the odd name Werner Eschholz zur Hohenburg. That was not his real name, but when I told him I planned to put him into a novel, he choose that name for himself!

HUBERT KENNEDY (b. 1931), formerly a professor of mathematics with a research interest in the history of mathematics, has long been interested in the early history of the gay liberation movement. His books include a study of the Swiss tri lingual gay journal *Der Kreis* and biographies of the Italian mathematician Giuseppe Peano, the German homosexual rights pioneer Karl Heinrich Ulrichs, and the German anarchist, writer, and boy-lover John Henry Mackay. Other publications relating to James Mills Peirce include:

The case for James Mills Peirce. *Journal of Homosexuality* 4 (1978): 179–184.

Towards a biography of James Mills Peirce. *Historia Mathematica* 6 (1979): 195–201.

James Mills Peirce and the cult of quaternions. *Historia Mathematica* 6 (1979): 423–429.

The first written examinations at Harvard College. *The American Mathematical Monthly* 87 (1980): 483–486.

James Mills Peirce, fierce & Quixotic ally. *Harvard Magazine* 85, no. 2 (November–December 1982): 62–64.

New England's first mathematical family. *New England Mathematics Journal* 16 (1983): 26–28.

www.ingramcontent.com/pod-product-compliance
Lightning Source LLC
LaVergne TN
LVHW041153080426
835511LV00006B/579